SELF-ORGANISED

Stine Hebert & Anne Szefer Karlsen (Eds.)

Open Editions

45 Handforth Road
London SW9 0LL
United Kingdom

+ 44 (0)20 7820 9779
info@openeditions.com
www.openeditions.com

Hordaland Art Centre

Klosteret 17
PB 1745 Nordnes
5816 Bergen
Norway

+47 55 90 85 90
www.kunstsenter.no

First published in London 2013

British Library Cataloguing in Publication Data:
A catalogue record for this book is available from the British Library

ISBN 978-0-949004-17-8

Printed and bound in Europe

SELF-ORGANISED

Occasional Table

Open Editions / Hordaland Art Centre

Julie Ault
Maibritt Borgen
Céline Condorelli & Johan Frederik Hartle
Anthony Davies, Stephan Dillemuth
& Jakob Jakobsen
Ekaterina Degot, Charles Esche & David Riff
Barnaby Drabble
Jonas Ekeberg
Linus Elmes
Juan A Gaitán
Abdellah Karroum
Livia Pancu
Jan Verwoert
What, How & For Whom/WHW

Stine Hebert & Anne Szefer Karlsen (Eds.)

Table of Contents

10 – 16

FOREWORD

Stine Hebert, Anne Szefer Karlsen
& David Blamey

DAVID BLAMEY My understanding of the term 'self-organised' within the art context is that it describes how groups, collectives, and other networks of individuals can operate independently from institutional and corporate structures. Self-organised initiatives appear to have strived to be non-hierarchical and conduct their decision-making processes along the lines of open participatory models. Some have developed counter-economic strategies as an alternative to traditional capitalist organisational principles that are perhaps, in the view of the self-organisers, exploitive or reliant on top down power dynamics. Was it your intention to reassess this commonly held view? Have you observed an evolution of the term, or a shift that warrants a re-appraisal?

ANNE SZEFER KARLSEN Many of these principles still apply, but we don't believe that looking at self-organisation as part of an opposing dichotomy is any longer possible. However, we started out with this opposition in mind. Our investigations have focussed on self-organisation beyond the limiting labels of 'alternative', 'non-profit' or 'artist-run', which have been the prevailing terms dominating discussions of both the subject and its history in recent times. Looking at self-organisation as merely a response doesn't take into consideration that the choice to be 'self-organised' implies a certain dualistic dependency, between the self – an individual – and an organised community within society. We see this dependency as being governed by common interest more than formality and obligation. The field of self-organisation is therefore more complex than the conventional separatist approach entails. It has moved beyond a process of simply dissolving boundaries between institutional and non-institutional platforms to creating new possibilities.

STINE HEBERT It should also be stated that we have deliberately focussed on self-organisation within the art world rather than as a general phenomenon in society. Self-organisation has otherwise been discussed primarily in social-political commentaries, such as in: *Self-Organisation/Counter Economic Strategies* (edited by Will Bradley, Mika Hannula, Cristina Ricupero and Superflex) from 2006, or in the reader on art and labour, *Work Work Work* from 2012 (edited by Jonatan Habib Engqvist, Annika Enqvist, Michele Masucci, Lisa Rosendahl and Cecilia Widenheim). Self-organisation is of topical interest at the moment and in 2012 alone we have seen the following publications come out: *Institutions by Artists* (edited by Jeff Khonsary and Kristina Lee Podesva) which documents a conference in Vancouver that aimed to evaluate the performance and promise of contemporary artist-run centres and initiatives; *Institution for the Future* (edited by Biljana Ciric and Sally Lai) presenting reflections by artists, curators and other cultural workers on what an institution for the future should and needs to look like; and *Artist Run Spaces* (edited by Gabriele Detterer and Maurizio Nannucci) focusing on artist-run spaces of the 1960s-1970s. One of our intentions has been to supplement these earlier discussions and so we have narrowed the focus and aimed at counterbalancing the existing works that historicise the subject of self-organisation by locating it within a limited geographical context, during a specific period of time.

ANNE SZEFER KARLSEN This anthology is also inspired by the recent surge of history writing in the non-institutional field. Increasing volumes of books and seminars have surfaced during the last couple of years showing an active engagement with the historicisation of the field by the very same people involved in it. An absence of competing accounts has allowed the practitioners involved to write themselves into history – ironically, often employing the same strategies as their institutional cousins. The resulting potential for self-mythologising projects that would otherwise be forgotten caught our attention and raised an important question in our minds: do the self-organised subjects of today situate themselves differently from the past and if so, how? Stepping back from the 'outsider' position seems to be an important determining factor and so we have also been interested in investigating the driving forces that make a non-institutional initiative transform itself into an institutional structure.

DAVID BLAMEY If you have detected that in some instances the purity of self-organised ideals being expounded in the late 1990s and early 00s have become corrupted, looking through the other end of the telescope, could it also be suggested that some art institutions have begun to adopt the methods of self-organisation, but perhaps without reforming their inner most intentions. If so, are there any particular examples that you could site that would bring this observation into focus?

STINE HEBERT In the spring of 2010 we were able to observe close at hand the celebration of the tenth anniversary of Tate Modern in London through the event, *No Soul for Sale – A Festival of Independents*, as both of us were invited to participate by two of the 'independents' that took part. This turned out to be a highly unconventional celebration of a museum's first decade of institutional service and on many levels a contradictory site in which to encounter so many non-institutions. Each of the 70 so-called independent initiatives that were invited to take part was assigned a demarcated space in the museum's Turbine Hall. The overall experience functioned as a kind of chaotic bazaar. Unfortunately the museum didn't offer any financial support to the contributors that participated in this celebration, and only minimal organisational assistance. The fact that most invited participants so readily accepted these terms demonstrated to us an important lesson about how the institutional art world sustains itself: the value of the institution's embrace still offers enough prestige and power to compensate for the problematic conditions on offer. However, we have to concede that this dependency is mutual, as the institution in this case desired to be associated with the energy and free spirit only found outside of its own heavy museum bureaucracy.

DAVID BLAMEY But this idea about a mutual dependency of conflicting interests could be seen as being an essential precept to the wider mechanics of art's production and consumption. Certainly in my lifetime there has always been a discernable link.

ANNE SZEFER KARLSEN Indeed. An example of a project that productively considers such a relationship would be the retrospective exhibition, *Trauma 1-11: Stories About the Free University in Copenhagen and the Surrounding Society in the Last Ten Years* at the Museum of Contemporary Art in Roskilde, Denmark (2011). Copenhagen Free University (CFU) was a project co-founded by Henriette Heise and Jakob Jakobsen in their apartment in the Nørrebro district, which was also the artists' home. Between 2001-07 CFU operated as a space for research and knowledge exchange. It hosted activities such as workshops, film screenings, lectures, small exhibitions and produced publications. Heise and Jakobsen developed the exhibition project *Trauma 1-11* in collaboration with Emma Hedditch, Howard Slater and Anthony Davies and it was conceived as a poetic representation of how the experiences of their practice within CFU and in society affected each other. The exhibition was presented as a 60-minute sound walk through the museum's spaces where the audience encountered propaganda material, props and remnants from the CFU as well as new works. The commentary leading the audience through the exhibition was transmitted through a recorded voiceover. It told the story of CFU's establishment in Heise and Jakobsen's home, recalled the reasons to cease activities, and explained how years later they were informed by the Danish government that it had become illegal by Danish law to use the term 'university' for anything but state authorised institutions. Presenting this kind of exhibition in a museum context raised some interesting questions about history writing and about what gets included, as well as excluded, from the archive. The exhibition provoked thoughts on the status of self-organisation on many levels and in particular, it emphasised one of our assumptions: that when an institution, or non-institution for that matter, decides *not* to cave into instrumental demands, that is the moment when the self-organised crystallises and becomes visible.

DAVID BLAMEY Two thoughts immediately come to mind from this example. Firstly, that this discursive method of working mirrors the rise of curatorial practices that have taken place over the same period. Secondly, that this CFU exhibition was mounted in the same year as your Tate example - presumably drawing from the same well of ideas, but with a strikingly different flavour.

STINE HEBERT Yes, these cases highlight very different approaches to collaborative work between non-institutional and institutional platforms. *No Soul for Sale* received harsh criticism for its barely-concealed exploitive undertones, while the *Trauma 1-11* exhibition proved to be a more productive example of a museum hosting an independent project's poetic exploration of its own history writing - with a result that was in fact empowering for both. Ultimately, the two exhibitions accentuate the gravity of mutual dependency that you make the argument for, in their own ways.

It's also true that the last twenty or so years have seen a blossoming debate on the development of curatorial practice. Discussions have necessarily taken place as a consequence of the gradual - one could also say inevitable - institutionalisation of the curator, as well as an increased segregation of discussions on conventional institutional and non-institutional structures. This tendency has manifested itself widely and can be observed in discourses dealing with curatorial practice, artist-run spaces, *kunsthalles*, biennials, art education, museums and of course, the development of institutional critique in all its facets. Our discussions have been closely linked to the development of the field of curating, but we have approached the subject of self-organisation without taking the curatorial as a starting point *per se*. Instead, our aim has been to open our examinations up for all contexts where art is commissioned, produced and displayed. Another question then that we would like to raise is about what the relationship between the self and community is. In this case between the individual, the art system and crucially, society at large.

DAVID BLAMEY So you are accepting of the idea that the art world – or our mainstream European province of the global art world – operates as a kind of matrix of independent and institutional positions, but in re-examining the presumption that these are somehow rival or conflicting standpoints, have developed a more holistic picture. One of the things that interest me here is the hint of communalism that's entering this discussion. When you talk about 'community' and 'society' in relation to the 'self', are you proposing that an analysis of the responses that you received from contributors points to the possibility of some kind of social transformation?

STINE HEBERT It is dangerous to claim that self-organisation holds transformative potential in itself – that could easily be mistaken for business management jargon and capitalism's vicious capacity to profit by absorbing the alternative. As Jan Verwoert's article expresses, the state of society today forces you to organise yourself – either on your own, or together with others. But this line of reasoning should not be mistaken for a situation based on total freedom. Rather, the urge to self-organise stems from the struggle to survive. It is a response to the political climate and all the implications of our changing economic situation. There is certainly an urgent need to take action and realise other economies outside of the capitalist production paradigm. A couple of propositions for this can be found among our contributors here: Céline Condorelli points at friendship as the core support structure for a better way of living; Barnaby Drabble speaks about the potential liberation of 'de-organisation' as the only way to change our over-managed lives; and WHW proposes to employ another temporality in our everyday life – waiting, not as a passive withdrawal, but rather as an insistence on allowing room for criticality to develop by testing out and gradually assessing new modalities for art production.

DAVID BLAMEY All of this raises a question in my mind about the continuing draw of institutional power, particularly since we are in a period where across all sections of society there is such a general lack of confidence in institutions, such as the banking system and the press. In the UK, our economic, social and political difficulties are seen as being linked to a general decline in institutional integrity.

STINE HEBERT In the seminal text from 2005, 'There is no alternative: the future is self-organised, part 1' (TINA), co-authored by Anthony Davies, Stephan Dillemuth and Jakob Jakobsen, the argument is put forward for the revolutionary potential of a future of self-organisation. The manifesto criticises existing institutional structures for operating by principles instigated by private corporations and for loosing sight of their public obligation. The authors thereby claim self-organisation as the only way to proceed from this point of departure. In the years passing from when this text was written, the financial crisis impacted as a global phenomenon and caused a total collapse of many large institutions. Following these dramatic changes in society, the trio has felt compelled to revise their text for this anthology and TINA2 speaks of self-organisation as a radical process that continuously challenges the fixed relationships our society is built upon - between the self, the individual and the institution.

ANNE SZEFER KARLSEN As curators and educators ourselves, working both independently and institutionally, we are actively involved in questioning the complicated relationships that underpin our work. The experience of moving between different platforms and operating with multiple voices has made the need to reassess conventionally fixed positions in the art world imperative at this time. The problem of how to position the self-organised within this paradoxical and changing environment has therefore informed the analysis within this book.

STINE HEBERT In asking writers, artists, art historians, curators, and critics as well as museum directors to present a singular take on self-organisation based on their own experiences, we have sought to analyse the topic using both empirical and theoretical tools. The diversity of this approach is intended to mirror the pluralism of the scene. We therefore begin with a group of contextual readings of the self-organised; this is followed by a series of case studies written by people who reflect upon their own activities over varying distances and times; and we conclude with more polemic statements that speculate about the future. Instead of getting bogged down by semantics this volume does not then attempt to map the territory and its historical development in the art world, but rather, it hopes to question and reorient an understanding of what it means to be 'self-organised.'

ON DE-ORGANISATION

Barnaby Drabble

OR, WHAT ONE CAN DO, WHAT ONE DOES, WHAT ONE AIMS TO DO, WHAT ONE ALLOWS TO BE DONE, HOW PRECISE AND DEFINED ONE'S AIMS ARE AT THE OUTSET, WHAT ONE REFUSES TO DO, WHO ONE REFUSES TO DO IT WITH, WHO ONE, IDEALLY, WOULD LIKE TO DO IT WITH, WHO ONE ENDS UP DOING IT WITH, WHY ONE DOES IT, WHY ONE IS TEMPTED NOT TO DO IT, WHY ONE THINKS ONE IS DOING IT, WHY OTHERS THINK ONE IS DOING IT, HOW, IN THE END, IT GETS DONE.

(1)

If, like myself, you are a fan of polemics, it doesn't get much better than Anthony Davies, Stephan Dillemuth and Jakob Jakobsen's freely distributed rant 'There is No Alternative: THE FUTURE IS SELF-ORGANISED'.[1] Neoliberal politics, corporations, managerial elites, the art market, and ultimately the museum and anyone who works within it, are ticked off here like a surgeon listing malignant tumours for urgent removal. At the heart of the text is the authors' call for the abolition of all art institutions on the grounds that they are socially and morally corrupt, and that they, like the governments that support them, are incapable of imagination, and deliberately ignorant of any forms of social organisation outside those prescribed by the demands of capital. In their eyes, even those critical souls who have collaborated with the institutions in the hope of changing them (and here they include themselves) are deluded, and should cease such collaborations immediately. The future, they proclaim, is self-organised.

But, if the future is self-organised, which definition of self-organisation are we talking about? At first glance this ever more popular term appears to have a broad range of connotations, even within the relatively refined context of the arts. Without overly getting into semantics, it is worth considering how these two words sit together in relation to any imagined future production. The 'self' in self-organised can be seen as operative in two ways: firstly it denotes the individual subject (him or herself), and, secondly, an idea of reflexivity (where the subject and object of an activity are identical). Similarly, the word 'organisation' has two applications: on the one hand as a process of bringing things into

1. Anthony Davies, Stephan Dillemuth and Jakob Jakobsen,'There is No Alternative: THE FUTURE IS SELF-ORGANISED', Part 1, in Nina Möntmann (ed.), *Art and its Institutions. Current Conflicts, Critique and Collaborations*, Black Dog, 2006, pp. 176–8.

order, and on the other as a group of subjects engaged in a common endeavour. In the light of these dual meanings, self-organisation in the arts has come to mean both a process of self-determined organising (as opposed to being organised by someone else) and an entity, an organisation of subjects created by the participants on their own terms (as opposed to one created for them to operate within).

Although radical in its call for an absolute takeover, 'There is No Alternative' upholds the traditional point of view that self-organisation is predominantly a tool for the little man with which to work in spite of, or in opposition to, the predominant system. In the arts the 'self' in question is frequently the artist, and for the most part the 'someone else' that commonly plays the organising role or provides the predetermined context for labour, can be identified as the institution, the museum, the market or the academy. In addition, a cloud of related terms hangs around the term self-organisation, referring to processes and structures that undermine, circumnavigate or critique the domination of culture by institutional and commercial agendas. 'Artist-run', 'independent curator', 'alternative space', 'bottom up', 'DIY', 'no-budget', 'open source', 'free school', 'counter public' and 'project-based', are just a few of these. Yet, if the departure point in the arts is frequently an 'us versus them' stance, the diversity of ideas in this small cloud of terms alone reminds us just how broad a spectrum of activities the term self-organisation has come to be applied to, a premise perhaps for the overall discussion of this publication about whether, taken together, these activities may constitute an institution in and of themselves.

(2)

Davies, Dillemuth and Jakobsen are fully aware of the looseness of the term they discuss and are quick to point out that self-organisation is too frequently, and, in their view incorrectly, equated with the plethora of home-grown initiatives that adopt the logics of creative entrepreneurship. As part of a lengthy passage, in which the authors point at the ways in which the term is misunderstood and misapplied, they argue that self-organisation 'should not be confused with self-enterprise or self-help, it is not an alternative or a conduit into the market. It isn't a label, logo, brand or flag under which to sail in the waters of neoliberalism.' Similarly, they dismiss established socially engaged artistic positions, and institutionally critical positions that none the less use the institution as an arena, declaring that these serve only to portray the 'sad farce, the vacant charade that passes for political action and engagement in the art system.' Whether we agree with their prognosis or not, it is interesting to see the authors placing issues of marketing and credibility at the heart of what they see as the problem with institutions. We might talk here of a crisis in the representative function of the traditional art institution, with 'representation' here to be understood not only in its socio-political, but also in its aesthetic sense. By noting the undeniable tendency towards brand building by the larger institutions and arguing that the politics within them have become a 'charade', the focus is brought to bear on the question whether these institutions have become so tied up in the 'business' of representation, and the expediency this entails, that they have forgotten to pay attention to the nature of the practices they are tasked to look after.

Today we are often told that institutional production constitutes a cultural 'offer', of which we can consider whether we wish to take it up or ignore. This idea of culture as an offer from the state is underlined by the 'use them or lose them' logic with which right-wing politicians are dismantling funding for many publicly funded arts organisations in Europe these days. Conveniently, this discourse is forgetful of the fact that it has been the citizens, by way of their tax and (in some countries) lottery tickets, who have indirectly given many of these structures life in the first place. Unconnected to this spend is the fact that culture is not something the state offers to us: quite the opposite, culture is inherently 'ours', emerging as it does through a creative process of interaction and collaboration between citizens, in relation to their environment. Those institutions that increasingly seek to crowd-please are at fault when they forget the fact that they are tasked with providing a space for public culture, in all its discursive complexity, and instead seek to represent culture 'to the public', in an easily consumable fashion. For such institutions, content (and here read 'arts practices') is required per se to reciprocate the agendas written up in their 'mission' statement. Only that which can be argued as compatible with their marketing strategy is given space. This back-to-front situation is a 'charade' indeed, a moment at which culture becomes a game of silently acting out trivial things, in order to pass the time.

In the light of this, the precise difference between self-organisation, self-enterprise, self-help and any number of other self-words (including self-interest) remains, in practice, remarkably hard to hold on to. At the heart of this problem is the fact that oddly similar individualistic ideas of the 'self' find themselves at the centre of radically different views of social reality, be it the discerning consumer self at the heart of the capitalist daydream (because you're worth it) or empowered revolutionary selves pitching their individual expression against the power of the state and the corporations (because I won't fall for their lies). To put it another way, the nature of self-organised activity often depends more on which particular self is doing the organising than on the activity itself. Human beings, inevitably, have a habit of screwing up the best laid of plans.

So, when the authors envisage 'an organisation of deregulated selves', which is 'at its core a non-identity' we should recognise, acutely at this moment, the clear need for art and its institutions to step outside the representational economic space that is increasingly prescribed for it within the political arena; the need to stop representing culture and actively provide a space for its production. Similarly, in suggesting that opposing what is happening is an 'organisational' task, we should identify that such an endeavour can only be undertaken when we do it together. Yet, at the same moment, the very term 'deregulated' reminds us of the double bind of the post-Fordist predicament. Only the deregulated stand a chance of imagining an 'outside', but while doing so they embrace a precariousness that makes them ever more reliant on, or at least at the mercy of, centralised, regulated systems. This is the paradox at the heart of the endeavour of self-organisation: in its truest form it is not only non-commercial but actively anti-profit in capitalist terms, and as such intensely incompatible with the current context of a growing cultural economy and move to immaterial labour.

Davies, Dillemuth and Jakobsen note this incompatibility and deal with it head on by entirely discounting the possibility of constructive work in any relation to the current seat of power, be that through diversifying the scope of the institutional frame or critiquing this frame from the inside. Instead they repeatedly argue for self-organisation as the tool for creating an 'outside' position: not as an alternative but as a successor to the institutional and commercial. This impresses, but also proves disingenuous. For both the brilliance and weakness of their text lies in its side-stepping of the paradoxical position of self-organised structures in the present moment, with their predicament of representing a phantom alternative to the all-encompassing effects of capital, while demanding public money. In what essentially resembles a revolutionary tract with state-managed footnotes, the authors imagine a future in which the institutions dissolve, but don't evaporate. Instead they rather handily leave a pool of public money for 're-distribution' to these self-organised bodies; a cultural utopia, this post-institutional world dispenses with the old order of publicly funded organisations while retaining plenty of no-strings-attached funding for the true and worthy in the arts community. Organisation, and the power position it denotes, is to be devolved to a set of people (and here they include themselves) who have other ideas about power and another way of organising themselves.

(3)

I am a curator, and, in keeping with this activity, have a congenital compulsion towards organising things. Over the years of working on exhibitions and associated cultural projects, I have become aware of just how much of my life I have spent working on funding applications, workflow diagrams, spending forecasts and strategy documents. Although, in practice, the production of these abstract constructions is only a part of my work, they play a defining role in what follows by literally prescribing my daily activities. It is these plans and the tasks they outline, which fill my diary with deadlines, my inbox with emails, my phone with new numbers and my to-do list with boxes to tick. All of this entirely underlines my existence as an exemplary post-Fordist, immaterial labourer (of the kind Davies, Dillemuth and Jakobsen so bemourn). Paradoxically, however, it is precisely these administrative trappings (the world of plans and meetings), albeit in the service of a kind of counter-bureaucracy, that are still to be found at work in successful self-organised structures. So in addition to any analysis of existent connotations of self-organisation in the arts, we might need to step beyond a debate about which 'self' is legitimately allowed to do the organising and into a critique of the rise of the 'organisation of the self'. By this I mean the increasing application of time and resource management methods to our personal lives, and the impact of this development upon culture as a whole.

Thinking of the readers of this publication, I am guessing that you, like myself, have been brought up to believe that planning, setting goals, making the 'right' decisions and putting in the hard work is the way adults should behave in the real world. Similarly, I am sure many of you have had that experience of being creatively booked-out, which I allude to above: a situation in which the problem has become one of displacement. The focus we have to give these days to the correct management of money, time and space, supplants other, indefinably valuable qualities that might live in the space between a project's conception and its completion. Despite their power to define, control, assure and persuade, ultimately the plan, the strategy and the budget in themselves seem to offer no greater promise to us than the pleasure of at some point being able to say: 'Well, we did what we said we'd do.' It is maybe this strong suspicion that something important is being lost in this process, that draws me to an appreciation of the kind of absolutist views expressed by Davies, Dillemuth and Jakobsen, because here too, in a supposedly 'creative' endeavour there is increasingly 'no alternative' to a stifling self-imposed bureaucratic approach. So, I currently find myself questioning what it might mean to simply lay down the tools one day and say: 'It's over, all of this is over, from now on, no more organising stuff.'

I am not suggesting that we stop working. After all, I chose this job and I know that as a curator I am expected to organise things: objects, people, ideas, resources and whatever else I can get my hands on. What I am contemplating is whether it is possible to reconsider the legitimacy of this expectation and its promise, in my context, of simply 'yet another exhibition'. Maybe the idea begins with a wish to start working from a sense of necessity rather than provision, and to replace planning with initiating and to start providing an impulse or starting point without claim to ongoing control. In many incidences experience tells us that the plan is most interesting when we allow ourselves to deviate from or ditch it, at best quite unexpectedly, for something different entirely. This is particularly the case when the plan was not ours in the first place. To enter into a polemic of my own, right now, I would argue that we need to call into being contexts for producing culture based on the ad hoc, the last minute and the improvised, with which we could adequately respond to the necessary. Although many would argue that self-organised initiatives can provide such contexts, I am not convinced they often do, precisely because they are not questioning the internal logics of organisation itself.

We live in a time of excessive organisation, in which the idea of 'order' has become overvalued, and in which conflict, in its political sense, is repeatedly circumnavigated in favour of consensus. In the light of this, all of us involved in the field of the arts might best invest in the dissolution of the concept of organisation altogether; both in the sense of 'putting things in order' with its administrative and systematic connotations, and of the 'group engaged in a common endeavour' with its suggestion of agreed aims and goals. We need to have the courage to stop organising things and to see what emerges, and the first step in this process for freelancers is to stop shoring up our craft in a rational and managerial way and to consider our own contribution to the institutional sector (whether state or self-organised) as exemplary of a different mode of production – which I will call de-organisation. To imagine the characteristics of this approach at the current time is difficult, because unlike other takes on organisation, it argues for the production of less rather than more. Less organisation for sure, but also less of everything else: less doing, less talking, less making, less thinking. De-organisation begins with switching off the overheated machine and relaxing to the sound of the decreasing hum as it slowly grinds to a halt. In the silence that follows, faith in the de-organised approach involves embracing those 'indefinably valuable qualities' latent within the process of working together on our culture that were mentioned before. We need to develop a sensibility and patience in the face of these abstract qualities, listen to them and let them guide our actions. It is only at this level that 'more' comes in: de-organisation involves more waiting.

(4)

To recap, any debate on whether the self-organised has become synonymous with the institutional cannot help but recognise the history of differentiation and antagonism between the two sides. This can be observed, as a fairly simple 'us' and 'them' logic based on who the 'selves' are, coupled with a ground-level incompatibility in relation to an idea of how power should be distributed. It is in this sense that the term self-organisation has become a rallying call for anti-institutional projects, often with little analysis of whether any real, operational differences exist between the structures developed by artists and those developed by the state or the market. In their rejection of institutions whose compulsion to 'represent' has effectively hollowed out their purpose, Davies, Dillemuth and Jakobsen intelligently point out the poverty of ambition of these spaces where our culture is essentially sold back to us in a 'lite' form. Their critique raises the question of what form or non-form we might find for initiatives that genuinely refuse to represent, avoid filling preconceived roles and refrain from standing in for any prescribed sets of social relations. Despite hankering after an 'organised' solution, the authors also point to the possibility that what they are trying to promote may be more 'spirit' than 'structure'. '[...] a tool that doesn't require a cohesive identity or voice to enter into negotiation with others. It may reside within social forms but doesn't need to take on an identifiable social form itself.'

What they appear to be alluding to is a power that is distributed and ambient, alive within forms, rather than busy authoring them, and, due to its heterogeneous and continually changing character, irreducible to any singular agreed upon statement of identity. Here is the germ of de-organisation in their imagined future, a subtle suggestion of what might arise from the dissolution of organisational hegemony, which appears at odds to their wish to 'take control'. In place of the organised it evokes a moment of trust in the ongoing life of something, without assuming responsibility for its planning. This also points to one aspect of the term self-organisation that is frequently overlooked in the arts and that complicates any overly simplistic reading of it as a tool for self-determination among artists. This is not the simple idea that artists can 'do it themselves', but instead, the more abstract idea that, left to their own devices, structures, including culture, may begin to organise themselves. To explain what this might entail, the definition of self-organisation used in the natural sciences is useful. In those fields the term describes the way in which particular natural systems have a tendency to develop, and take new and more complex forms, in a seemingly unplanned fashion, without the influence of an external or central authority. In such cases, changes in the nature of the whole system occur on account of numerous actions at a low level, with the smallest parts interacting locally without the need of an overall view of the whole. This is what scientists who analyse systems have come to call 'emergence'.

It may appear dilettantish to suggest that we should communally place more trust in the intangible and unfathomable aspects of 'how things come to be'. Practically speaking it would be, in so far that these are things that we cannot preconceive, which therefore lie outside the realm of the organised. But, meditations of this kind are important, because, on the face of it, the cult of professionalisation and the resulting equations of better organisation, quality and transparency have had an increasingly stultifying effect on our museums and academies in recent years. This is having the same effect as excessive performance feedback and employee monitoring in business and our own stress-inducing predilection to remotely steer all aspects of our lives from our laptops and iPhones. Even if I am inclined to worry about a future art world that is self-organised by the likes of Davies, Dillemuth and Jakobsen, in which I am quite sure I would be led to the guillotine for my long years of collusion with the enemy, I have to agree in part with their diagnosis of today's institutions: most are 'failing in their task'. But, the truth of the matter is that there is simply no time or space in our organised lives to look again at what this task might be, or ask sensibly whether cultural work is really about tasks at all. Equally, it is time to face the fact that there is no neoliberal bogeyman forcing us to do things this way and no cabal to overthrow. In fact, if we draw from a comparison of the institution, the organisation and the individual today, we see, more disturbingly, that we are doing this to ourselves; we are willingly ushering in an era of self-imposed micro-management that borders on the institutionalisation of the self. Maybe, in the spirit of dilettantism, it is time to reassess the benefits of a life less organised.

27 – 36

THERE IS NO ALTERNATIVE: THE FUTURE IS (SELF-) ORGANISED PART 2

Anthony Davies, Stephan Dillemuth
& Jakob Jakobsen

Reclaiming Self-Organisation

Part one of our text, 'There is No Alternative: THE FUTURE IS SELF-ORGANISED' (TINA1), was first published in 2005, a period when the 'animal spirits' of unlimited accumulation were still drunk on their own sense of infallibility. At the time, we couldn't fail to notice a similar over-confidence and arrogance in the attitude of the political, managerial and professional classes that were moving deeper into cultural and educational institutions.

We therefore felt unsure about accepting an invitation to speculate on self-organisation by an institutional commissioning body that had only recently staked a claim in this tendency and its discourse. The organisation in question, the Nordic Institute For Contemporary Arts (NIFCA) had itself become vulnerable when the progressive programming for which it had become internationally renowned fell out of sync with the increasingly localised and insular interests of its political backers. Without broader consultation it was closed in 2006 – its funds redirected to a more 'manageable' organisation without significant public opposition or protest.

In TINA1 we sought to rethink self-organisation, a term that had gained currency as a means to disguise organisational restructuring, manage critique and enhance professional careers. The text sought to place self-organisation back within its oppositional and revolutionary vocabulary, also setting it off against 'self-help' and 'self-enterprise', terms with which self-organisation had become confused and whose tendency was to stabilise and extend rather than challenge institutional hegemony.

That was 2005 – a world away – before the systemic contradictions started to become more pronounced and exploded with such frequency, and with such blinding force and violence, that the animal spirits faded, the image of eternal growth was shattered and, for most, the ruins beckoned.

The Coming Resurrection

In the midst of a period of intense struggle, violence and social upheaval, who needs economists and pundits to remind us that this is the worst financial crisis since the last? As bad as the 1990s, 1980s, 1970s, the late 1920s? Isn't the evidence all around us all the time? In the intensities of labour struggle and workers' suicides in China and South East

Asia, the further dispossession of the poor in the US, or the punishing effects of austerity measures imposed everywhere, particularly in those neoliberal European economies once regarded as exemplary, like Greece, Italy and Spain.

For decades, the catastrophic consequences we now find ourselves living through were deferred by fostering rapid market expansion and contraction, boom and bust. Here, crisis played an integral part in the seductive, syncopated rhythm of 'creative destruction'. Bust was deferred by selling it as boom – which no doubt displayed a certain creativity. A formula of almost redemptive proportions was devised to cover up the wreckage while the supposed necessity of uninhibited free market expansion could be relied upon to sanction even the most blatant acts of global plunder. In tandem, novel ways of shifting, shunting, bundling and repackaging otherwise problematic phenomena, allowed *everything* – even debt and poverty – to continue to serve capitalist accumulation.

An early response to the financial collapse of 2008 was the slogan 'We won't pay for their crisis', which later gave way to the more trenchant statement 'Capitalism is Crisis'. This underlined the realisation that the most vulnerable are not only paying a high price for the crisis, but that crisis is implicit in a system where such violence, such destruction is part and parcel of its reproduction. A distinction must here be made between economic and ideological crisis. The former is integral to the logic of capitalist accumulation, which in its neoliberal mode has contended that 'free' markets have a tendency towards self-regulation and can therefore construe crises as a temporary manifestation of that principle. The latter is a consequence of the former; a rupture in the *belief* in capitalism compounded by deep social crisis. The more established middle classes, for example, have been thrown into self-doubt, having lost their sense of global hegemony and the material securities they took for granted for decades. The world's poor, meanwhile, are, as ever, pushed further down into the mud.

It is this congruence of the economic *and* ideological crisis, which has exacerbated misery everywhere – and, with it, conjured potentially revolutionary forces now appearing on the surface. As the ranks of the newly immiserated and proletarianised continue to swell, the former middle classes now sit cheek by jowl with those whose hopes of escape they may have once embodied.

But could it be said that this re-composition is part of a more generalised revolutionary process? What we see instead is that the coming resurrections of zombie tendencies are already fully compliant with capitalist logic: nationalism, populism, xenophobia and an obsession with security – to be flanked by propaganda, surveillance, dictatorial, and/or mafia type structures.

Disciplinary austerity is presented as a necessary corrective, an emergency response to the economic crisis and global market crash Should that fail to convince, there's always the tale of 'public sector over-spending' and 'living it large' – a popular profligacy to justify the collective sacrifice. After all, 'we're all in this together'. These narratives are typical of capitalism's meagre offering of legitimating excuses.

Under the Wheels

In recent decades we have seen a very close integration of market dynamics and culture. We have witnessed the rise and rise of the Creative Industries. These promised the liberation of Marx's alienated workers in a process of creative self-realisation and autonomy. Through creativity of the hands and the hearts, they would grant capitalism a human face. Artists, with their idealism, flexibility and enthusiasm to work even under precarious circumstances, became the role model for a new concept of capitalism, leading its 'triumphant procession around the globe'. The hopes for this spectacle were twofold: it would strengthen belief in capitalism's new formula, and it would disguise the fact that, like so much else wealth generated under the sign of creativity, it was the product of a proliferation of speculation, and increasing indebtedness. Meanwhile, under the procession's grinding wheels, the sweatshops, child labour, privatisation of commons and all other disasters that accompany the economic warfare of rich versus poor, continued unabated.

As workers in the cultural and educational sector we have to acknowledge that what passes for critique and politicisation, particularly within the contemporary art community, has proven to be even more toothless than feared. Mimicking the strategies of corporate management, art institutions adopted the rhetoric of social responsibility and ethical governance as a means to appear progressive. Under the guise of art trends like relational aesthetics and the new institutionalism, and state agendas like social inclusion, the privileged continued their merry dance.

Political agendas were de-politicised, struggle was taken out of politics as glamorous institutions dressed up as community centres, and corporations as charities. While this may not have entirely convinced the progressives and radical reformists, they still singularly failed to expose a deeper process of de-structuring, organisational hollowing out and the consolidation of existing power relations.

With the recent economic collapse, and the ideological crisis of capitalism, the more progressive branches of the cultural institutional landscape entered a void, displaying both panic and paralysis. In some cases institutional surfaces became more porous and open, while in others they congealed and contracted further, becoming ever more rigid and conservative. At the height of the Occupy Wall Street movement, New York's Artist's Space, for example, demonstrated how both processes can occur simultaneously. Here, management initially supported its own 'occupation' by artist-activists. But the progressive dream scenario of participation 'from below' suddenly turned undesirable, when 'lack of clear demands' was cited as cause to call security and remove the occupiers from the building.

In 2008, similar institutional confusion and violence marked the 28th São Paulo Biennial, where the ground floor of the massive exhibition complex was left open 'for the community'. When urban graffiti crew, *pixadores*, entered the space with their spray cans, as might be expected, they were forcibly evicted by security and police. This was not the right kind of 'participation'. Students of Berkeley University occupying Wheeler Hall in 2010 fared no better: faced with nothing more than a sit-down protest, Administration called the UC Berkeley police, which used pepper spray to drive the students from their institutional home violently.

Where antagonisms are not successfully negotiated or suppressed, institutions tend to lay low – either reproducing the state narrative that the crisis is an anomaly that can be overcome, or quietly scrambling for ways not to be cut or shut.

If we can be sure of anything at this moment, it is this: there will be no bailout for us. In fact, it is much worse – communities, homes, workplaces and organisations have again been called upon to facilitate the next phase of capitalist development. The question is: what are we going to do about it? Which is only interesting insofar as it could equally be, what can we do about it? That is, while we remain subject to a system geared towards squeezing cash even out of the rubble it generates, the task, as we see it, is to remind ourselves that this rubble might offer a relative but significant opening: namely an awakening sense that there is no neoliberal future to build, and that we're no longer compelled to compete as individuals for a piece of the free market world. Against this backdrop, we can measure those in the art system as it stands and by what it is they have to offer in the preparation of a post-capitalist society.

Race to the Bottom

It remains urgent to examine how institutions learnt to simultaneously demand their subjects (workers, students, consumers) accept less (wages, resources, support) while having to pay more (fees, free and voluntary labour). This would include the intensification of 'hollowing out', where institutions outsourced large swathes of their activity bar the baseline cultural programming, which continued to legitimise their existence. And, more recently, the rhetoric of 'de-institutionalisation', which, removed from its original context of mental health and community care, gained some currency among art professionals as part of a pragmatic institutional response to austerity agendas.

The bogus consultative mode associated with this discourse is now widespread, demonstrating that an increased 'openness' to exterior (and critical) forces can alleviate the immediate impact of dwindling funds and gaps in programming by effectively securing free input into everything, from content to strategic organisational development. By way of illustration, London's ICA, on the verge of collapse in late 2009, gathered representatives from the 'critical art community' for an invitation-only discussion forum, The Reading Group. Its framing questions, albeit generalised, clearly also possess a strategic function: 'What work can we do?', 'How do we find alternative ways of thinking about production and labour?' and 'How can we act collectively?'

How, then, do we begin to relate the material impact of the 'race to the bottom', which can be seen everywhere - all competing against all, all the time - with what appears to be a personal and simultaneously institutional need for, and indeed desire to, cooperate, work together, self-organise? To counter this apparently unassailable dynamic, we must continue to define the system's key characteristics and patterns, especially as these develop and change. Do we have any choice but to ally ourselves with the explosive rage this has triggered on the streets, directed so decisively at symbolic sites of knowledge, wealth and power?

What role do cultural and educational institutions play during this period of rapid change? Given the current scale of cuts and devastation, these places, where some of us happen to work, study, breathe, pose an unenviable choice: do we self-organise, break the relationship, fight it out among the ruins and accelerate the process of collapse, destruction? Or do we take on more traditional forms of opposition, slow down the process in the search for a temporary haven in the violent storm? These questions follow us into the ruins, a crumbling landscape where the terms may have changed, but the struggle, which remains a class struggle, continues.

As we move into the ruins, can art production, the art system and its institutions, for example, play a part in unlearning capital? C an it feature in a more generalised process of de-education and unlearning? Can it contribute to the exit, the movement out of capitalism? Can those in the cultural and educational sector situate notions of collectivity and communism beyond the specialisation that capitalist production continues to impose? Can these struggles be connected, widened? Can they contribute to post-capitalist, de-specialised spaces, which enable cultural production and engagement in the wildest sense?

Those of us with a need to continue to self-organise will do so in relation to the specific contours and tempos of our respective struggles. Some of us self-organise because we still can, and because we have no choice, while some self-organise to survive, to resist. Self-organisation relies on a dominant form of organisation only to depart from it. Whether it's workers on the factory floor or artist revolutionaries elsewhere, the desire to self-organise is first and foremost caught in the contradiction that it both affirms and breaks with the dominant order. If we, then, accept that self-organisation serves a specific purpose at a specific point in any given struggle, we might also ask: at what point is it possible to move beyond self-organisation? And what would this 'beyond' look like?

Into the Ruins

There is no reason to be afraid of the ruins, among which some of us now find ourselves, because they could represent the end of capitalist relations and the dissolution of its opaque administrative bodies. It's difficult to feel concerned about the ways in which the term self-organisation has been re-purposed by those who rely on its aura of radicality to prop up their ailing power. The desired outcome of self-organisation is not the affirmation of the self, the individual, the institution – it's in the negation of these relationships.

Take over the factory (again!), occupy the schools, colleges, universities, hospitals, rip up management dictats, diss reforms, take over all public transportation, dismiss self-help, head-lock entrepreneurs, outflank the bosses, cancel all dodgy contracts, drop ownership, turn over directors, managers, curators, administrators, break into their offices, liberate their 'resources'.

In all its forms, self-organisation is a basic and necessary social process that relies on an initial binding condition or problem, which is then addressed collectively. It is a collaborative tool, a means to mobilise skills, experience, support, resources and knowledge. Looking back (and forward!), we see its role in the formation of council democracies (soviets, Räte, councils), where politics developed at the level of the factory, kindergarten, neighbourhood – and people came together to organise, practically, artistically, intellectually.

But it should be noted that decision-making and debates about executive and legislative processes can produce larger, more complex structures – a union of councils. In order to gain broader impact for different experiments in self-organisation, it will eventually become imperative to join forces, organise and unite beyond various specific and singular interests.

Issue impossible demands, make no demands, say nothing, deny everything, wreck classrooms, put social knowledge to work, re-deploy those wasted years of education, construct new tools, question and undermine normalisation, tear apart populism and nationalism, take space, refuse reform, refuse negotiations, refuse explanations, no demands in their language, anti-normative, anti-hegemonic, pain in the ass, fragile, refuse their language, scream, shout, dance, riot, smash, fuck, make noise, remain silent.

As we've seen in recent struggles, it is necessary to work against the tendency to cut off self-organised processes from a potentially revolutionary mainstream in order to gain momentum. The framework and infrastructures for such connections are everywhere, at all times. But how can they be brought together in such a way as to maintain 'difference', and allow for tensions, antagonism and disputes to be productive? In the process of its own negation, then, self-organisation should continue to question terms like consensus, alliance, solidarity and democracy.

Try out, flow, keep on, moving with others, enjoy failure, camps, communication, interaction is production, rewrite history, redefine identity, unlearn property, make demands in another language, redistribute the sensible, de-specialise, re-specialise, re-imagine the present, socialise depression, make new dictionaries, vocabularies, lexicons, indexes, catalogues, new maps.

Continuing to produce culture, despite the dominance of capital and its institutions, is not a call for a placebo utopianism, or to prepare for a separate form of life outside of production and the creation of surplus. Instead, it means testing new forms of collaboration and developing a different measure and grasp of value. Here, production embodies mutuality, togetherness, new and dynamic social relations, all of which continue to occur among the ruins, helping to accelerate the expansion of the commons and a total transformation of social relationships.

Block, parry, side-step, strike, counter, dig out, confront, tear up, get your shit together, your guts together, boycott, complete dissent, proletarian shopping, hit and run, critique, purge, find unexpected comrades, abolish, destroy money, watch the bullshit fall apart, dance among the ruins.

A key task now is to derail capitalist restructuring, continue to widen the cracks, block all attempts at reform wherever possible. We need to build, protect and defend the communes and commons that will make up post-capitalist life. As we've seen, most states and their institutions can switch into emergency mode at a moment's notice, unleashing levels of extreme violence that are commensurate only with their own fear - not with any actually existing threat. New warfare is underway everywhere - on the Internet, in the street, private and public sphere; all are either in a state of emergency, or threatened by impending incursions. We have to maintain the alliances and continue to develop the destructive language that shapes the exit.

Merge, get organised, disorganise, flow together, join forces, exchange experiments, experiment with yourself, get rid of yourself, slowly, start synthesising, synchronising, syncopating, shaping structures, play with weapons, stray research labs, converging forms of communication and collaboration, anti-property, no-property, property-less, non-proprietorial, non-patriarchal education, self-educate, co-educate, experiment, dump your expertise, experiment, no programme, force open the archives, inhabit histories, dig the bones out of the rubble, re-animate the long, long memory of political struggles, victories and defeats, activate conflicting utopias, realise oneiric knowledge.

END

'There is No Alternative: THE FUTURE IS SELF-ORGANISED'
Part 1, June 2005, can be found here: http://societyofcontrol.com/llibrary/culture/davies_dillemuth_jakobsen_TINA1_future_selforganised.htm.

37 – 49

THE INNER AND OUTER FORM OF SELF-ORGANISATION

Maibritt Borgen

Today we are witnessing a growing interest in self-organisation as a curatorial, artistic and institutional practice; a shift that the publication of this book in itself demonstrates. But what is the foundation we use when we discuss whether we are witnessing an 'institutionalisation of self-organisation'? What historical period do we assign self-organisation to, and how, if at all, do we theorise it? Is it a strategy? A mode of survival? A lived practice, best maintained in a safe exile outside any art-historical framework, or an example of collective cynical opportunism?

Self-organisation is a mode of practice and a term founded in a self-conscious narrativisation of de-central collectivity and the dissolution of modernist hierarchies. Self-organisation has around twenty years of history in the context of Denmark, where it has played a significant role in the development of contemporary art. Anthologies and exhibitions often put a global perspective on self-organisation, but having recently moved from Denmark to the United States has made me aware that self-organisation should not be talked about in global terms. Motivations, possibilities and relationships to state and authority deviate too much to allow for specific political articulations to become clear. What I propose, then, is rather to try and unravel a sort of 'micro-history' of the development of the term and practice in a Danish context; a micro-history that is in many ways representative of shifts on a global scale.

Self-organisation as a mode of practice comes accompanied by the development of self-organisation as a term, which describes a new development in collective practices from the 1990s to the present day. Here, practice grows out of discourse, and vice versa. I limit my use of the term self-organisation to the last twenty years from the belief that the collective practices prior to this period were not strictly self-organised in the way we understand the definition today. Rather than existing within a pluralistic discourse those involved then perceived themselves as posing alternatives to the hegemonic, political order.

The plurality of practices and motivations that characterises the contemporary field has created a need for a critical re-evaluation of the term. Since the 1990s, the term has moved away from the original essentialist sense of that of anti-capitalist critique. It has become intertwined with a general development in post-industrial society that has absorbed self-organisation to a state in which the term has come to include a variety of practices, ranging from exhibition collectives and social activism to Internet communities. I want to ask if we – the art historians and the cultural practitioners – in this plurality still know what self-organisation essentially *means*? In an attempt to track this development, I will describe self-organisation and the rhetorical development of the term, how it became implemented in artistic practice, and how current shifts in practice have in turn influenced its use to a situation in which it has become necessary to speak of self-organisation as having two forms: an inner and outer one.

Self-organisation is inscribed in the model of the 'rhizome', a term used by by Gilles Deleuze and Felix Guattari in their postmodern opus *A Thousand Plateaus* (1980) to describe the production and movements of desire in contemporary society. The rhizome is derived from the world of botanics, and is most easily understood as a system structured like the multitude of roots in grass:

> 'Unlike a structure, which is defined by a set of points and positions, the rhizome is made only of lines [...] the rhizome pertains to a map [...] that is always detachable, connectable, reversible, modifiable, and has multiple entryways and exits and its own lines of flight [...] all manner of "becomings".'(1)

In the rhizomatic condition, strategies, negotiations of power and relations are constantly changing. It is a structure that priveleges sideways ordering and movement over centre-periphery relations, and one needs to think only of the Internet, post-industrial production and contemporary warfare to understand how this affects society. The rhizomatic world produces a myriad of small narratives, a multi-form production that influences critical artistic modes of organisation. Resistance too must become multi-form to exist in this rhizomatic society, as the agents of power constantly change, and re-negotiate their positions. Self-organisation becomes established as a term under the conditions of a rhizomatic society. The term originated in the 1970s and 1980s, when the changes of post-war society led to a rhizomatic condition, and previously solid institutions like the nuclear family and firm ideologies were shattered. It was also a time when the belief in the possibilities of collective organisation from 1968 began to vanish and change under the new neoconservative paradigm. The word itself is not confined to the art world, but describes in more general terms a

1. Gilles Deleuze and Felix Guattari, *A Thousand Plateaus*, Continuum, 2004, p. 21.

shift in scientific epistemology from centralist to de-centralist behaviour. It describes the patterns of closed systems and the way in which independent systems interact and produce spatial, temporal or functional structures without orders from any central governing body.(2) These systems '[...] acquire their new structure without specific interference from the outside; i.e systems that are self-organising.'(3)

Self-organisation as a model can be used to explain behaviour in everything: from flocks of birds to traffic. When used in connection to contemporary art and cultural practice, I would claim self-organisation describes practices in which two or more individuals decide to work collectively in a temporary and flexible structure. Self-organisation surfaced as a discourse around art in the early 2000s, but is descriptive of collective practices beginning in the 1990s. These practices were organised in a way that reflected the synergetic metaphor of systems that increased in complexity and produced new knowledge 'without interference from the outside'.(4) Autonomy from the governing powers of society was the goal.(5) Danish artist collective N55 started out as a studio collective set up by students from the Royal Danish Art Academy in the mid-1990s. But in a short amount of time they developed into a collaborative live-work entity of four people whose lived practice experimented with modes of autonomy that would provide independence from capitalist society.

Towards the 2000s, self-organisation was on the one hand given an increasingly anti-capitalist and political dimension, propelled by the spirit of the anti-globalisation movements of the 1990s, the rise of the Internet and a new, theoretical paradigm, in which network-based action was given ever more critical weight. Working in a self-organised way was increasingly perceived as potentially the only response to a new political reality, in which multinational entities, rather than national governments, were seen as the enemies. The flexibility of self-organised practice resonated with the critical writings of philosophers such as Michael Hardt and Antonio Negri, whose ideas of the resistance of the 'multitude' replaced older subjects such as people and class. The main claim was the need to create a new political subject, not unified in a collective subjectivity, but a collection of

2. Igor Yevin, 'The Synergetic Approach to Art Theory: Recent Investigations', in *Leonardo*, Vol. 27, No. 5; and 'Prometheus: Art, Science and Technology in the Former Soviet Union', Special Issue, *October*, 1994, p. 213.
3. Hermann Haken, *Information and Self-Organization – A Makroskopic Approach to Complex Systems*, Springer, (third edition) 2006.
4. Ibid.
5. Will Bradley, Mika Hannula, Cristina Ricupero and Superflex (eds.), *Self-organisation/Counter-economic Strategies*, Sternberg Press, 2006.

singularities. The goal for critical action was to take part in spontaneous protests rather than joining a political party, etcetera.

When governed by what Deleuze and Guattari call 'lines of flight', a subject is enabled to move rapidly and painlessly from one plateau to another. A constant set of negotiations is therefore inscribed in the rhizome, creating a potential for self-organisation as a form of resistance that could escape being assimilated into the centre of power. As a realisation, the term came to incorporate specifically an increasingly multi-faceted catalogue of practices, which felt united against a global network of power relations. These power relations were seen as the conglomerate of art institutions, the advertising industry, multinational corporations and the capitalisation of creativity performed by copyright law, hegemonic conceptions and all other actors that in one way or another influenced artistic practice.(6) Because of this bodiless, hard to define enemy, the term was given a plurality in the following definition, put forth by Danish artist collective Superflex, one of the most high-profile Danish self-organised groups, in 2006:

> 'In recent years it has been used in relation to certain kinds of social groups or networks; in this context, the term does not have a strict definition, but broadly speaking it refers to groups that are independent of institutional or corporate structures, are non-hierarchical, open and operate participatory decision-making processes.'(7)

This definition pluralises the term because an anti-capitalist critique is embedded implicitly, but it is also characteristic of the undefineability of the term: it is easier to define what one is not, than what one essentially is.

Simultaneous to the politisation of the term, which presupposed an alignment with anti-capitalism, another historical development unfolds. In this shift, working self-organised becomes about a collective work mode indebted to spontaneity, shifting the term inclusiveness to the level of form rather than that of motivation. Curator and critic Mika Hannula characterises self-organisation as follows:

6. 'There Is No Alternative: THE FUTURE IS SELF-ORGANISED'. Available online at http://www.societyofcontrol.com/llibrary/culture/davies_dillemuth_jakobsen_TINA1_future_selforganised.htm
7. Will Bradley et al, op. cit., p. 5.

'an abstract phenomenon ... a meeting of different, often collaborative forces, but also conflicting desires, wishes and fears ... a transaction, a kind of platform, or an intersection of flows of information, capital, attitudes, amusements.'[8]

Hannula's statement describes self-organisation as a potential, as an articulation of an undefined 'something', made possible by the open, participatory character. If this is taken as a basic definition it becomes a working method that seems to need no motivation except for the method itself. This lack of emphasis on political justification, which is prevalent in Superflex's definition, turns self-organisation into a self-sufficient working mode, and has far-reaching implications. Self-referentialism on this level suggests that self-organisation has an inherent criticality: that things are supposed to be critical because of the sheer fact that they are self-organised. A critical development that raises the need to speak of two modes of self-organisation: self-organisation as an inner and an outer form.

The term self-organisation took over from older (but still widely used today) terms to describe collective practices, primarily labels such as 'artist-run' or 'alternative'. These collective practices, which emerged in Denmark from the 1990s onwards, were started by a new generation of increasingly internationally oriented artists, who were labelled the 'International Underground'.[9] Working as self-organised collectives became a way of seperating themselves from older generations, from the a-political attitude of the 1980s and what they saw as the failure of so-called alternative practices.[10] It was a change caused by primarily two motivations. First, younger artists associated themselves less with the local history of collective organisation in artistic practice, and more with international movements in art.[11] They also did not perceive artists as belonging to a professional class with specific demands regardless of generational divides. They did not feel that the demands and concerns of

8. Will Bradley et al, op. cit., p. 207.
9. This is described more thoroughly in writings such as Ann Lumbye Sørensen, 'Kunstbase Alfa - Den Polyfone Strategi', in Anneli Fuchs and Emma Salling, *Kunstakademiet 1754-2004*, The Royal Danish Art and Architecture Academy Press, 2004; Rune Gade and Camilla Hjalving, *Nybrud - Dansk Kunst i 1990erne*, Aschehoug, 2006; as well as the thesis by Ida Vesterdal Jørgensen, *Den Internationale Undergrund [The International Underground]*, handed in at the Centre for Cultural Studies, Media and Communication, University of Southern Denmark, 1999.
10. Rune Gade and Camilla Hjalving, op. cit.
11. Ida Vesterdal Jørgensen, op. cit.

their generation were answered by the established structures of artistic organisation. Denmark has a long history of artists working collectively, originating in the nineteenth century with the artists' associations. For many years, these were the primary mode of organisation for young artists.[12] In the 1990s, these associations had obtained relative power on an institutional level and had themselves become gatekeepers, which made it hard for a new generation to gain influence.[13] Because of this shift, the idea of the artist-run as a critical gesture in and of itself lost its validity. Furthermore, what challenged the idea of the artist-run was that the artists felt increasingly connected to a contemporary global generation of critics and curators, and had no intention of excluding these from being involved in their modes of organisation.[14]

Secondly, the idea of art providing alternatives to contemporary society in and of itself seemed increasingly impossible. The idea that art could change the world was seen as a failed, political position, primarily because it had become too close to a critique of an institution that had changed so much it could incorporate any critique. Art's emancipatory potential was as a consequence put in a state of crisis, as it was in danger of being reduced to pure gesture. The new sense of a collective work mode was intellectually indebted to changes caused by 1960s art and cultural activism, even if artists were critical of their impact. Self-organisation in the 1990s and 2000s reflected 1960s collective practices, but the artists involved believed that rather than launching a true, critical potential, many of these alternative structures had disappeared or moved to the centre of culture, and become institutions themselves. This sentiment is reflected in the words of American artist Julie Ault, who in 1996 characterises the alternative arts movement in New York as a thing of the past, confined to the years between 1965 and 1985, and its current situation as the 'disintegration - perhaps even obsolescence - of an alternative art sphere'.[15]

12. With Den Frie Udstilling [The Free Exhibition], the first artist organisation in 1851.
13. As an example, the Artist Associations have secured equal representation in several governing boards.
14. Exhibition spaces like OTTO (1997–2001) and Globe (1992–96) are good examples of this cross-professionalisation.
15. In her 2002 book *Alternative Art New York*, which builds on an exhibition she curated at The Drawing Center in New York in 1996. The exhibition was funded by the state agency NYSCA, and asked a range of artists and cultural practitioners to 'evaluate and assess the alternative arts movement'. The disillusion she felt at the time she later modified. Ault's accounting of a local New York history can be compared to a Danish context because the 1990s generation to a large degree defined itself globally. This is evident when reading artists' publications and catalogues from this period.

But what were these alternatives that were seen as failed? The rebellious decade of the 'long' 1960s in Denmark was, as elsewhere, a rich cultural period of collaborative models for work, new cross-genres, and initiatives that breached the line between artistic and social practice. The early 1960s paved the way for preoccupation with new forms, internationalisation and cross-disciplinary practices, and, as the decade unfolded, art gradually moved into the larger social sphere. The Experimental Art School, founded in Copenhagen in 1961, among others broke new formal grounds, and Gallery Köpcke, founded by the German artist Arthur Köpcke, attracted an international crowd of artists.[16] Art was linked to the women's movement, not only on a larger ideological level, but with smaller, yet significant initiatives such as establishing daycare facilities at the Royal Danish Art Academy, which enabled female artists to continue working when they became mothers.[17] Art merged with anti-Vietnam activism through street theatre and happenings, artists' working conditions were addressed and a union adressing artist' rights was formed.[18] Solidarity practices and community engagement merged in art.[19] Increasingly artists abandoned the art institution altogether and joined the general mix of hippies and anarchists in experiments with new ways of organising life in squats, communal living and self-organised communes.[20]

All these were essentially 'alternatives', in that they saw the institutions of society as functioning in one way, and themselves focusing in another. The people involved felt that their own micro-gestures had potential for adressing larger political issues, and that they encompassed a utopian element and a way of imagining a different society and another way of structuring production. They worked on two levels, which

16. The groundbreaking Fluxus Festival in the Nikolaj Church, Copenhagen, 1962, was to a large extent an international event that shocked the local audience. Kanonklubben [The Canon Club] (1968 -) started out as a camera collective among students at the Royal Danish Art Academy, named after a Canon video camera, but evolved into an autonomous department run by the students.

17. Significant events included the exhibitions 'Damebilleder' [Ladies Pictures] In 1970 and 'Kvindeudstillingen' [The Womens Exhibition] in 1975, as well as the founding of a student-run daycare facility at the Royal Danish Art Academy.

18. Billedkunstnernes Forbund (BKF) [Association of Visual Artists].

19. Tøj Til Afrika (TTA) [Clothes for Africa].

20. The independent communes Project House and Christiania formed in Copenhagen. Away from the city the independent community farm Stålvængegaard, the hippie commune Det Nye Samfund [The New Society], and an alternative farm on the small island Livø were all signs of this significant new development.

informed each other: the everyday pragmatic and the ideological. And art was seen as a powerful tool for affecting change.[21]

The writings on self-organisation do not reflect the same beliefs. This does not mean that many self-organised initiatives, which were able to move beyond the frame of relational aesthetics, did not have a critical conscience. But they did not to the same degree fuse the everyday pragmatic with the ideological.[22] Instead, their belief rested on the establishing of networks, cells and the transmission of knowledge.

As the self-organised collectives abandoned the term of alternatives, the institution started paying attention. In the new millenium, global cultural institutions increasingly started to operate on market terms, and every critical gesture would fast be incorporated in the institution,[23] in what I would label a new 'economy of critique'.[24]

As a consequence being self-organised lost its anti-institutional stance. In the words of Gilles Deleuze, we are currently living in a 'society of control' in which institutions are no longer easily perceived as buildings of brick and stone, but rather as a complex set of power relations that humans internalise and reproduce voluntarily and willingly.[25] Or, in the words of American artist and critic Andrea Fraser, who herself is considered a key character in the second wave of Institutional Critique, it is no longer possible to be anti-institutional, as the art institution is essentialy everything and everyone who recognises art as art. Instead of defining themselves as alternatives to established institutions, then, the new social practices took a different path in defining a critical position, such as when Danish collective N55 tried to establish the political responsibility of the artist with the statement that 'art is about meaningful relations between things and their surrounding world', which emphasises art's engagement in a physical reality, and thereby in the world.

21. In 1975, the later professor at the Danish Art Academy Albert Merz wrote about The Womens Exhibition at Charlottenborg, that the exhibition was based on a 'human case we are all involved in'.

22. Claire Bishop has been one of the foremost critics of relational aesthetics, especially in her paper 'Antagonism and Relational Aesthetics', *October*, No. 110, Autumn 2004, pp. 51–79.

23. One sees this very explicitly in a project like Copenhagen Free University founded in 2001.

24. In 2006 Danish artist and founder of Copenhagen Free University, Jakob Jakobsen along with German artist Stephan Dillemuth and English cultural activist Anthony Davies, all with a long track record in critical, cultural practice, sent out the manifesto 'There Is No Alternative: THE FUTURE IS SELF-ORGANISED', in which they pleaded for 'reducing uncertainty' and self-organisation.

25. As Gilles Deleuze described in his text 'Post-script on the Societies of Control', printed in the Danish artist magazine *Åndsindustri* [Spirit Industry] in 1992.

Self-Organisation as Outer Form

After the 1990s and the subsequent boom in the contemporary art market, self-organisation in many ways became a model of working, and a training ground for young artists within the Danish art world.[26] It became an *outer form*, not an *inner necessity*, through which the artists envisaged themselves as agents for change in society. Today, art has moved even further from a place in the margins or in opposition to society to a place in the centre of what society desires. In the words of Danish art critic Lars Bang Larsen: it has even become a powerful force for creating desires in society.[27] This already began in the mid-1990s, when artists were seen as contributors to the GNP in a new creative economy and the visual art were seen as a powerful tool for national branding.[28] This perception was helped by two doomsday bibles Larsen also singles out: Pine and Gilmore's *The Experience Economy* (1998) and Richard Florida's *The Rise of the Creative Class* (2002). State support fast picked up, incorporating neoconservative strategies into criteria for funding.

Self-organisation shares many features with the contemporary labour market, in which features such as flexibility, dedication and creativity are increasingly sought after. Self-organisation today in many ways connotes the perfect worker, and within the visual arts we are increasingly faced with a new 'economy of critique', that can turn the self-organised into profit. Self-organisation became what the system wanted, in many ways, and today it has become an established mode of practice within cultural institutions at large – a change that is illustrated by an ever-increasing list of symposiums, panels, talks and 'critical interventions'. All these events simultaneously operate in a self-organised way within an institutional discourse and thus give critical legitimacy to the institution. The success or failure of these must thereby be judged by their mode of interaction and their level of self-critique and consciousness.

This historical move is the determining factor for what I choose to label as a situation in which we now have self-organisation as outer form. The groups and collectives that work 'self-organised' today are

26. Tom Jørgensen, 'At løfte i flok' [Sharing the task], in *Kunstavisen*, No. 10, November/December 2005; Ida Vesterdal Jørgensen, op cit.
27. In his publication *Art is Norm*, Jutland Art Academy, 2009.
28. The Danish Minister of Culture referred to this in her speach for the students at the Royal Danish Art Academy in 1995, and several reports published by the Ministry of Culture analyse how art and business can work together.

many. They range from those practices that most think of as being self-organised – theoretically founded or critical public and local practices that aim to engage with the role of the artist in society – but increasingly also encompass a range of exhibition collectives, which seems to aim equally for a share of the market and for a critical point. The term also includes essentially web-based artist communities and practices that exist in close relation to the market. In their anthology, Superflex ascribe artistic self-organisation to a global catalogue of resistance practices: from cooperative factories in Argentina to Superflex's own projects such as the open licence softdrink Guarana Power.[29] But it is not a given that self-organisation has a critical autonomous position. Rather, the task must be to engage with the plurality the term now contains and use this to re-locate and re-define their criticality.

A Critical Agonism

Contemporary western capitalism is failing rapidly as any look at the news on the current recession and the Euro crisis will demonstrate. The Occupy movement is growing stronger, even under pressure, as is a widespread call for civil disobedience against the greed of the financial sector. Under neo-liberalism, artists' organisations were haunted by a sense that every critique could be incorporated, and that the only way to react was to not react. Still, the lines of flight we inhabit in a rhizomatic world are tools for an extreme speed and flexibility, and inherent in this flexibility lies also the possibility to rethink political change. The idea of rooting contemporary art practice in a world view in which one does not accept the institutional norm can – in a positive way – be to refuse its claim to power, but – in a negative way – it might as well not be adressing the power relations in which it is inscribed. There has been much critique of the varied forms of resistance that came up in the early twenty-first century. One valid point was that it was merely creating its own, counter-cultural market and not challenging established structures. At the fore of these critiques was the claim that a new generation of activists lacks the desire to work for long-time political change within the political system

29. See www.superflex.org.

of parliamentary society, or that they simply do not think in terms of systemic change altogether.[30]

Self-organisation is a notion that describes an independent reaction in complex systems, but the total decentralisation of these systems is not necessarily a given. Traffic flows according to a system of roads. Workers organise according to a larger scale of production. We must reclaim this long-term pragmatic political goal, and we need to figure out a way to move 'tactically' in the world, in the sense of how Michel de Certeau saw everyday life as a site for subversive practices. We must re-acknowledge the dominant structures of the art world, however they seem to have changed, and question the foundations for our institutions and how we work within them. Challenge, not exile, is the answer to creating a new political reality.

Following on from this, the increasing individualism of our times is often regarded as a threat to critical practice. In her 2010 article 'FREE' in e-flux journal, Irit Rogoff concluded that there might also be a potential in this singularity:

> 'Singularity provides us with another model of thinking relationality, not as external but as loyal to a logic of its own self-organisation. Self-organisation links outwardly not as identity, interest or affiliation, but as a mode of coexistence in space. To think knowledge as the working of singularity is actually to decouple it from the operational demands put on it, to open it up to processes of multiplication and of links to alternate and unexpected entities, to animate it through something other than critique or defiance.'

Along the same lines, Belgian philosopher Chantal Mouffe advocates that we need to re-animate the political sphere through plurality. To her, plurality is the foundation for a critical, political sphere, and this becomes possible when we recognise our political opponents. Very often self-organisation is characterised by what it is not; anti-capitalistic, anti-hierarchical etcetera, and I wish to speak against setting up these binaries. Mouffe advocates for an 'agonistic' democracy, in which political enemies are not seen as adversaries, but as equal political partners. She provides a framework for a political sphere that takes pluralism and

30. A development described by, among others, Joseph Heath and Andrew Potter in *Nation of Rebels: Why Counter-Culture Became Consumer Culture*, Harper Business, 2004.

mutual recognition of opponents as its foundation, a foundation we utilise, and through the rhizomatic create new political demands.

What I have been hinting at throughout this text is the fact that along the lines of self-organisation as a practice, a split has occurred in the term: a split that makes it problematic to engage with self-organisation in an institutional context. That self-organisation today takes on an *inner* as well as an *outer* form, and rather than being institutionalised, it is now being aesthetisised.

It is not unexpected that there is a return to the self-organised within the visual arts and cultural production in the current precarious situation. Art is, as always, a reflection of its sociopolitical reality. Self-organisation in an artistic and critical practice is born out of a globalised and subsequently pluralistic position, and the current political situation in many ways calls for a return to older notions of collectivity. But if collectivity is only returned to as a nostalgic model, it will omit critical reflection on its own condition. Maybe we need to embrace, rather than deny, our current individualism. The current urgent task seems to be to fuse the prevalent individualism and identity politics with a return to modes of organisation that can promote long-term political change and go beyond the singular protests at COP 15, Wall Street, and the student protests in London. A new mode of organisation that can form a bridge between the changed conditions of the art world, the art institution and the world at large is needed. For I believe Andrea Fraser is right when she claims that we can no longer be outside the institution. Can our position on the inside then become a way of demanding a new set of ethics?

50 – 61

INSTITUTIONAL EXPERIMENTS BETWEEN AESTHETICS AND ACTIVISM

Jonas Ekeberg

For this anthology I was invited to re-evaluate 'new institutionalism', a concept I introduced rather offhandedly in the book with the same title in 2003. Although this is not a full historic account of the various practices and theoretical debates that surrounded the field of institutional reform in the first decade of this century, I hope to be able to discuss a few crucial issues with more distance than was possible ten years ago. Specifically, I would like to look at the way in which new institutionalism became a prism through which the difference between an open-ended, aesthetic criticality and a more specific, anti-capitalist activism became apparent. *New Institutionalism* was the first publication from the then new cultural exchange institution Office for Contemporary Art Norway (OCA), and the term was both descriptive and normative from the outset.[1]

On the one hand it was meant to describe a number of art institutions that were, as stated in the introduction, 'adopting, or at least experimenting with, the working methods of contemporary artists and their mini or temporary institutions, especially their flexible, temporal and processual ways of working.' Several institutions were mentioned in the introduction, but the Rooseum in Malmö was seen as offering the clearest example. The director Charles Esche was quoted, saying that the Rooseum was becoming 'an active space [...] part community centre, part laboratory and part academy'.[2] In her historical account of the Rooseum, the Swedish curator Åsa Nacking describes Esche's period at the institution as follows:

> 'The Rooseum became a research centre for new art, where the process was made visible. In the exhibition hall studios for artists were set out, to enable the visitors to meet the artists and follow their work. An exhibition could just as well consist of the shooting of a film as of a regular screening. [...] Concerts, film screenings, talks, and performative events were integral parts of the activities, and cooperation between both regional and international groups was given priority.'[3]

On the other hand, new institutionalism was also a normative term, albeit in an ambivalent way. It carried some hope and enthusiasm for

1. Jonas Ekeberg, ed., *New Institutionalism*, Office for Contemporary Art Norway, 2003.
2. Ibid., p. 9.
3. Åsa Nacking, 'Rooseum and the condition of possibility', in Katarina Stenbeck, ed., *There's gonna be some trouble - The five year Rooseum book*, Rooseum Center for Contemporary Art, 2007, p. 21.

a renewed art institution as well as the ironical scepticism with regards to the fact that institutional critique was about to become co-opted by the institution itself, not only ideologically (as it had arguably been since the 1970s), but also practically, as a way of working.

Some commentators have proposed that new institutionalism was a Scandinavian or social democratic phenomenon, and this does perhaps hold some truth.[4] In spite of the rise of neoliberalism, the welfare state grew in many northern European countries in the 1980s and 1990s. This included an increase in public spending on culture, thus forming the economic and perhaps also ideological basis for new institutionalism in northern Europe.

New institutionalism did perhaps carry the slightly romantic belief that it was possible to both deconstruct and reconstruct a public institution from within in one and the same move. However, with the toughening political climate in Europe, this basis for experiments and developments turned out to be happening in a more precarious state than previously envisioned. As social democratic Europe met the opposition of right-wing populism, many contemporary art institutions came under fire.

What's in a Name?

Already at its inception, the term 'new institutionalism' and the field of institutional reform was heavily debated. The optimistic view that contemporary art needed a new type of institution and that this new institution carried an aesthetic and a political potential, was met with the fear (or the insight) that the development of an experimental art institution would be to the disadvantage of artists. This concern was already voiced by the critic Rebecca Gordon Nesbitt in the original publication:

> 'One of the main pitfalls with this way of working is that artists and their activities are forced into a construct defined by the institutions that generally serves to flatter the institution and disempower the artists.'[5]

4. See for example Alex Farquharson, 'Bureaux de change', *Frieze*, No. 101, September 2006.
5. Rebecca Gordon Nesbitt, 'Harnessing the Means of Production', in Jonas Ekeberg, op.cit., p. 84.

Criticism was also coming from art historians, who feared that new institutionalism in its rejection of the traditional exhibition model threatened to establish a new orthodoxy. The British curator Claire Doherty feared that new institutionalism would force contemporary art into a 'social' regime:

'how to respond to artistic practice, without prescribing the outcome of engagement; how to create a programme which allows for a diversity of events, exhibitions and projects, without privileging the social over the visual?'[6]

However, the most crucial criticism levelled against new institutionalism came from a new generation of Marxist critics. The Austrian philosopher and art theorist Gerald Raunig stated that 'new institutionalism' sounded like 'new public management', and by extension also other such concepts linked to the neoliberal state.[7] Raunig seemingly rejected the critical potential in the term and also the critical potential in the way the art institution adapted to 'the flexible, temporal and processual'. This was, on the contrary, seen as echoing that which sociologists Luc Boltanski and Eve Chiapello had dubbed 'the new spirit of capitalism', e.g. the most sought-after resource in post-Fordist capitalism.

Even though the term might be rejected, the discussion on new institutionalism was a welcome opportunity to focus on the relation between artistic production, public institutions and social change. As an alternative, Raunig proposed the term 'instituent practices', thus linking the field of changing art institutions to social movements and activism, rather than individual artistic practices.[8] Other radical curators and critics also discussed the changing field of art institutions by proposing alternative names for it: Jorge Ribalta referred to his practice at the Barcelona Museum for Contemporary Art (MACBA) as 'new institutionality', Charles Esche talked of his various projects as 'experimental institutionalism', and the artists Andrea Fraser and Hito Steyerl spoke simply of an 'institution of critique'.

6. Claire Doherty, 'The institution is dead! Long live the institution! Contemporary Art and New Institutionalism', in *engage review*, Issue 15, Summer 2004, p. 1.

7. This view was voiced by Raunig at the seminar '(Re)Staging the Art Museum' in Oslo in 2009.

8. Gerald Raunig, 'Instituent Practices – Fleeing, Instituting, Transforming', in *Transversal – Multilingual Web Journal*, No. 1, 2006, http://eipcp.net/transversal/0106/raunig/en.

This multitude of descriptive terms certainly signalled that new sites of cultural production had emerged and that it was imperative to discuss potentials and pitfalls. However, it also highlighted a significant opposition between aesthetic and activist positions in contemporary art theory.

Out of the 1990s

A history of institutional and museological experiments could start with the Salon des Refusés in the nineteenth century, but significant reform from *within* an art institution was probably first carried out by Alexander Dorner, director of the Landesmuseum in Hannover in the 1920s and 1930s. His radical exhibition policy - juxtaposing art with other objects of different periods - put him in direct opposition to the Nazi party.[9] However, the specific roots of new institutionalism as I discuss it here probably dates back to the 1990s. If we look at the Nordic countries specifically, there was a great dissatisfaction with the art institution among young artists in this decade, and as the neo-conceptual and social art practices of that generation started to be recognised by critics and collectors, the museums and art centres necessarily had to follow suit. The Louisiana Museum for Modern Art outside Copenhagen mounted the exhibition 'NowHere' in 1996, in which the figure of the international curator was fronted in a way that had not been customary in the Nordic countries until then. The Nordic Institute for Contemporary Art (NIFCA) hosted the seminar 'Stopping the Process' in 1997, asking international curators to stop for a moment to reflect upon 'the strategies and tactics of contemporary exhibition-making'.[10] Many others could be mentioned, and institutions like Witte de With in Rotterdam and KunstWerke in Berlin both adopted the rhetoric of the 'laboratory' (KunstWerke) and the 'experimental and flexible' (Witte de With) in the early 1990s. However, it was not until the turn of the century with institutions such as the Rooseum in Malmö (directed by Charles Esche between 2000 and 2004), the Palais de Tokyo in Paris (co-directed by Nicolas Bourriaud and Jerôme Sans between 2002 and 2004) and the

9. See for example the Dictionary of Art Historians, http://www.dictionaryofarthistorians.org/dornera.htm.
10. Maaretta Jaukkuri and Anders Kreuger, 'Foreword' to Mika Hannula, ed., *Stopping the Process - Contemporary views on art and exhibition*, NIFCA, 1998.

Kunstverein München (directed by Maria Lind between 2001 and 2004) that this impulse formed into a more coherent cultural movement.

The political component of this movement, at least in many of its early configurations, can easily be located in the 'relational' and subversive 1990s, what has also been dubbed the 'post-ideological' decade. The French curator Nicolas Bourriaud has been named the ideologist of this decade, and even if he is more concerned with the work of art than the institution of art in his much-referenced book *Relational Aesthetics*, the field of new institutionalism fits his description of contemporary art perfectly:

> '[...] it is no longer possible to regard the contemporary work as a space to be walked through [...] It is henceforth presented as a period of time to be lived through, like an opening to unlimited discussion.'[11]

Bourriaud linked relational art to urbanism, leaving its political outcome open:

> 'Art is the place that produces a specific sociability. It remains to be seen what the status of this is in the set of 'states of encounter' proposed by the City. How is an art focused on the production of such forms of conviviality capable of re-launching the modern emancipation plan, by complementing it? How does it permit the development of new political and cultural designs?'[12]

Bourriaud does envision a resistance to capitalism and consumption, but he arrives at this political stance through an aesthetical argument revolving around the way art produces forms of sociability that question capitalist consumption.

Another crucial aspect of such an 'aesthetic institutionalism' is highlighted in Swedish curator Maria Lind's title of the essay 'Learning from art and artists'. Here, Lind describes various mobile and experimental projects for the Moderna Museet in Stockholm in the late 1990s, confirming that the aesthetically attuned curator will always put artistic practice first. The result is a position characterised by openness and ambiguity:

11. Nicolas Bourriaud, *Relational Aesthetics*, les presses du réel, 2002 (1998), p. 16.
12. Ibid., p. 15.

'Contemporary work [...] is about scepticism and enthusiasm, affirmation and critique at the same time. While the older generation "broke the ice", so to speak, with its confrontational polemic stance, today it is easier to be more nuanced, smart, and sensitive.'(13)

This was written in the year 2000 and marks the turn of the century in more than one way. The projects Lind looks back on are from the late 1990, and her talk of 'affirmation and critique' also seems to belong to the previous decade. Only a year later, Charles Esche brings a new political dimension to the discussion, as he introduces his programme for the art centre Rooseum in Malmö:

'Now, the term "art" might be starting to describe that space in society for experimentation, questioning and discovery that religion, science and philosophy have occupied sporadically in former times. It has become an active space rather than one of passive observation. Therefore the institutions to foster it have to be part-community centre, part-laboratory and part-academy, with less need for the established showroom function. They must also be political in a direct way, thinking through the consequences of our extreme free market policies.'(14)

While building on the same experimental ideas as Maria Lind does, Esche has added the crucial dimension of direct, anti-capitalist critique. Even if Esche did not mention it explicitly, this coincides with the rise of various social and counter-globalisation movements at the turn of the century as well as the ideology of the same movement as described in the seminal volume *Empire* by Antonio Negri and Michael Hardt, published in 2000.

NIFCA notably took a similar 'political turn' a few years later with projects such as 'Capital – It Fails Us Now' (2005), 'Populism' (2005), 'Self-organisation/counter-economic strategies' (2006) and 'Rethinking Nordic Colonialism' (2006). For a while, NIFCA carried both the formal experiments of the 1990s and the radical politics of the 2000s to such an extent that director Cecilia Gelin claimed that 'one can actually say that we are working in a utopian art institution!'(15) However, Gelin must

13. Maria Lind, 'Learning from Art and Artists', in Brian Kuan Wood, ed., *Selected Maria Lind Writing*, Sternberg Press, 2010, p. 249.
14. Charles Esche, 'What's the Point of Institutions Like the Rooseum', in *Rooseum Provisorium*, No. 1, 2001. Quoted from Katarina Stenbeck, op. cit.
15. Cecilia Gelin, 'The Utopian Institution?', in Nina Möntmann, ed., *Art and its Institutions*, NIFCA/Black Dog Publishing, 2006, p. 6.

have been well aware of the meaning of the word 'utopia' as she went on to announce, in the next sentence, that the institution was about to be closed down. As we shall see, this was a deeply political decision, carried out by the cultural politicians from the rising right-wing Nordic populist movement. Together with the closing down of the Rooseum a year earlier, it marks a preliminary end point for new institutionalism in the Nordic countries.

The Activist Impulse

Activism was aesthetically represented in many art exhibitions of the 1990s (often emblematically, in the form of banners), and slowly it began to inform the practice of the art institutions more directly. The Rooseum and NIFCA were two Nordic examples, but MACBA in Barcelona had developed a similar approach already since before it opened in 1995. Under the directorship of Manuel J. Borja-Villel (1998–2007), MACBA engaged closely with various local political groups. In his account of the period, curator Jorge Ribalta mentions the workshop 'The Direct Action as one of the Fine Arts' in 2000 as a starting point. He states: 'Rather than social processes being given an aesthetic makeover or deactivated, this generated a newly created collaborative space in which the Museum began to form part of social struggles.'(16)

With the phrase 'giving social processes an aesthetic makeover', Ribalta explicitly refers to Nicolas Bourriaud, and thus reinforces the opposition between an aesthetic and an activist position:

> 'Nicolas Bourriaud's relational aesthetics corresponds to a superficial, soft and falsely consensual conception of artistic experimentation, which is actually immobilist and regressive in that it "aestheticises" the immaterial communicative paradigm and its implicit social and creative processes, imposing an expository regime that interrupts their mobility, and freezes and makes fetishes of practices.'(17)

Bourriaud defends himself against this vigorous attack in an interview in the Swedish art magazine Site, where he talks about the invention

16. Jorge Ribalta, 'Experiments in a New Institutionality', in Manuel Borja-Villel et al., eds., *Relational Objects - MACBA Collection 2002-2007*, Museu d'Art Contemporani de Barcelona, 2009, p. 239.
17. Ibid., p. 252.

of a 'non-radical opposition'. Referring to the works of Felix Gonzalez-Torres and Gardar Eide Einarsson, Bourriaud states that 'the artworks that are the most subversive are the ones who elaborate their content from forms and procedures — not the ones that repeat messages.'[(18)]

The activist impulse was most rigorously explored theoretically by the research organisation called the European Institute for Progressive Cultural Policies (EIPCP). Under the editorship of the earlier mentioned Gerald Raunig, the EIPCP started their string of investigations into the changing art institution in 2001 with the project 'kunst 2.0'. This became the starting point for the larger project 'republicart' in the period 2002–05, as well as the follow-up 'transform' in the period 2005–08. These projects included both theoretical investigations and various art projects investigating the possibility of a new politics in art. Under titles such as 'Precariat', 'Alternative Economics', 'Do you remember Institutional Critique?' and 'Progressive Institutions', Raunig and authors like Boris Buden, Brian Holmes, Marius Babias, Paolo Virno and Simon Sheikh, developed an idea of a political art institution formed in the image of the emergent anti-capitalist movement.

Art Against Empire

In the manifesto for 'republicart', published in 2001, Gerald Raunig formulated this programme for an art institution geared towards social change. He used the term 'multitude', referring to the conglomerate of oppositions to globalised capitalism as envisioned by Hardt and Negri in *Empire*. In Raunig's manifesto, the art institution is thus included in the ethos of 'a multiplicity of public spheres, not imagined statically, but rather as the becomings of articulatory and emancipatory practices'.[(19)]

In the 2004 essay 'What is a Progressive (Art) Institution?', Raunig answers the question of how an art institution can become part of such a political multitude by making use of Michel Foucault's concept of 'parrhesia', derived from the Greek for 'speaking the truth'. Raunig envisions an art institution that performs a 'double parrhesia'; of both criticising the power and disclosing the truth about its own position. In Raunig's view, it is not enough for the art institution to be self-critical

18. See *SITE*, No. 28, 2009.

19. Gerald Raunig, *republicart Manifesto*, 2002, http://republicart.net/manifesto/manifesto_en.htm.

and experimental, it also has to be critical of 'the power' – read globalised, neoliberal capitalism and governmentalism.

Raunig goes on, like Ribalta, but perhaps contrary to curators like Maria Lind and Nicolas Bourriaud, to link his institutional project directly to political and social movements:

> 'This link will develop, most of all, from the direct and indirect concatenation with political practices and social movements, but without dispensing with artistic competences and strategies, without dispensing with resources of and effects in the art field.'[20]

Here we arrive at what seems to be the logical conclusion of the activist position, that the art institution is an instrument in the service of social change. The artistic side of the matter is simply something that one should not 'dispense of'.

The German curator and critic Nina Möntmann arrives at the same instrumental view. In her 2007 article 'The Rise and Fall of New Institutionalism', also published with EIPCP, she looks for 'perspectives on a possible future' for the art institution. Here, Möntmann points out that many of the 'new', 'reformed' or 'progressive' art institutions of the early 2000s had seriously diminished or vanished completely before the end of the decade. Central to our discussion is that both the Rooseum and NIFCA closed down, in 2006 and 2007 respectively. In both cases, the advantageous conditions created by social democratic cultural policies were turned on their head as populist politics and neoliberal governmental reforms hit the Scandinavian countries. These ideological cutbacks have often been disguised behind administrative or economic arguments, but the effect has nevertheless been that there are fewer spaces for critical art practices. After squarely declaring new institutionalism as over, Möntmann arrives at her vision for the future:

> 'a conceivable new institution of critique would be one that maintains and expands its participation in (semi-) public space, and at the same time creates free unbranded spaces and negates dependencies.'[21]

20. Gerald Raunig, 'Instituent Practices – Fleeing, Instituting, Transforming', Ibid.
21. Nina Möntmann, 'The Rise and Fall of New Institutionalism – Perspectives on a Possible Future', in *Transversal – Multilingual Web Journal*, No. 08, 2007, http://eipcp.net/transversal/0407/moentmann/en.

Here, public space is – like the art field in Raunig's argument – simply there, something you can choose to participate in or not, while the 'free unbranded spaces' are the ones awarded agency. This simplified view of the public sphere, combined with a slightly romanticising attitude towards alternative spaces, is perhaps characteristic of a western art discourse that does not really believe in the political potential of its institutions. But, as Möntmann herself has pointed out, these institutions are in a precarious condition. Perhaps the political potential of these art institutions is their very existence. In which case, the public sphere and its art institutions is not simply something we can use or choose to participate in: it is something we must fight for.

However, according to Möntmann, there is another political solution to this problem that needs to be taken into consideration. A solution, we could add, that has followed new institutionalism like a shadow. What if one were to give up on the art institution and simply establish alternatives on the outside? 'No,' Möntmann concludes, 'the conclusion cannot be [...] to leave institutions completely aside in order to enter alternative spheres.' However, she struggles with this issue as she does not find much hope in the European art institution, where 'criticality didn't survive the "corporate turn".' Instead, she points to community-led projects in Delhi, Mumbai and Jakarta in order to find the kind of 'participatory institution-forming activities' that she idealises.

Seven years earlier, Maria Lind had asked a similar question, but from an aesthetical point of view: 'Does this kind of contemporary art even need the institutions at all? Can this art not communicate directly with the audience? Have the institutions become redundant?'[22]

Both Möntmann and Lind, as well as Raunig, conclude positively that we *do* still need the art institution. The question of leaving the institution, what political theorist Chantal Mouffe has called 'the exodus approach', does, however, arise again and again. This makes it impossible not to ask why is it that these commentators raise this question, just to reluctantly answer that they would like to continue their work within the institution. And, similarly, why does the question of defending the art institution not come up more often? Is it simply so that it is academically more comfortable to romanticise the alternative and the revolution, disregarding the political struggle to uphold existing public institutions? Well, it certainly looks like it, but the truth is – perhaps

22. Maria Lind, op.cit., p. 245.

paradoxically – that the very same people who disregard the art institution in theory are the ones who defend it in practice. The real problem has been that the art sector at large has failed completely to mount a defence for the art institutions under threat. Institutional Critique has left the defence of the institution impotent.

If there is something to learn from this for curators and commentators close to the alternative art institution, it is perhaps that their criticism of the art institution has been confused with their way of defending it. Thus, it has been difficult for the specialist and general audience alike to come to the rescue of places like NIFCA and the Rooseum.

In an essay in *Artforum*, Mouffe takes issue with 'the negative way public institutions are perceived by the mode of radical critique fashionable today':

> 'Instead of deserting public institutions, we must find ways to use them to foster political forms of identification and make existing conflicts productive. By staging a confrontation between conflicting positions, museums and art institutions could make a decisive contribution to the proliferation of new public spaces open to agonistic forms of participation where radical democratic alternatives to neoliberalism could, once again, be imagined and cultivated.'(23)

One such way forward could be to foster institutions that let the aesthetic and political impulses in contemporary art coexist under the same roof. This could also be a way of staging the kind of 'agonistic' public sphere that, again, Chantal Mouffe has advocated elsewhere. I think the most relevant – and radical – art institution of today would stay open and available, both to a general audience and to political activists. For what would be the purpose of political activism if it were not to share the space and the faith with a general public?

23. Chantal Mouffe, in *The Museum Revisited*, *Artforum*, Summer 2010

62 – 73

TOO CLOSE TO SEE: NOTES ON FRIENDSHIP, A CONVERSATION WITH JOHAN FREDERIK HARTLE

Céline Condorelli

The following text addresses the practice of friendship, as a specific entry in relation to the large question of how to live and work together towards change, as a way of acting in the world. Being a friend entails a commitment, a decision, and encompasses the implied positioning that any cultural activity requires. In the context of self-organisation, friendship is perhaps at its most evident in relation to a labour process, in *how we work together.*

I have been engaging with what I call *support*, which I consider essential to cultural production, for some time.[1] Friendship is a fundamental aspect of personal support, a condition of doing things together that deserves substantial attention, and is in many ways the missing chapter to my book *Support Structures*.[2] Friendship, like support, is considered here as an essentially political relationship of allegiance and responsibility. One of the best definitions of cultural production is perhaps that of 'making things public': the process of connecting things, establishing relationships, which in many ways means befriending issues, people, contexts. Friendship in this way is both a set-up for working and a dimension of production. In addition, working together can start from as well as create forms of solidarity and friendship, which are then to be pursued as both condition and intent, motivating actions taken and allowing work undertaken. The line of thought that threads through the following text therefore, is that of friendship as a form of solidarity: friends in action.

It seems appropriate to tackle friendship, itself a relationship, in the format of a dialogue, here taking place between philosopher Johan Frederik Hartle and myself. A chance encounter led us to develop an unexpected conversation on the subject over several months, mostly via email, which forms the basis of this text. While philosophy is the field in which friendship appears as a subject, it also holds the word friend (philía) in its very name, so the two are intimately and inextricably linked. The conversation, however, is articulated from our particular respective positions, that of an artist and that of a philosopher, between two practices that produce in different registers, even though they might sometimes share similar concerns. Our practices are usually differentiated between making and thinking, while making is also a form of thinking, and thinking is, undeniably, a way of making. These two positions produce

1. See the long-term project *Support Structure* with Gavin Wade, from 2003 to 2009, www.supportstructure.org.
2. Céline Condorelli, *Support Structures*, Sternberg Press, 2009.

different questions, and, of course, answers, that open up friendship as a productive concept and proactively ask the question: what can friends *do*?

There are many ways of working together, and it is important to put one's own practice in a constant relation to acting in public in the world at large.

My practice, like that of many others, often involves putting fragments in relationship to each other, so that the cumulative sum of these things - words, ideas - somehow proposes something that each part alone could not; through this I speak, not so much through an individual authorial voice, but through a multiplicity of voices. I find my position by collecting and navigating through material, and I try to make work that speaks in the same way, that works by articulating a complexity of material, explicitly in both form and content.

Perhaps this is a way of working that creates close ties and connections between things, people, and myself, and more often than not this feels like a friendship of sorts. I work by spending time with things I have collected, with the references that I carry along, with the numerous voices - of friends, acquaintances and peers - that are part of the process of developing work, which also include the essential voices of inspirational thinkers from the past that populate our thoughts and conversations and are thus also present. Friendship, then, is perhaps a condition of work. It might never be the actual subject of the work - however close it is to a long-term object of my practice, *support* - but it is a formative, operational condition that works on multiple, simultaneous levels.

With this particular awareness in mind, I recently started visiting the small, but rich philosophical discourse on friendship - through Aristotle, Montaigne, Derrida, Agamben and Blanchot - and found it is a discourse on friendship among men. Derrida addresses this problem in one chapter of *The Politics of Friendship*, and yet the issue remains: no female philosophers have written about friendship, to the best of my knowledge, and, more crucially, there seems to be something inherently patriarchal, perhaps fratriarchal about these constructions of friendship. They are closely linked to notions of freedom and democracy that come from the idea of nations of brothers (and the terrifying consequence that we can only live together because we are the same, we share the same land, the same birth, the same blood, the same language). Simple, haunting questions emerge from this: can I use a discourse that excludes me, and, if so, how?[3] Should I produce my own? And how would a discourse on friendship that includes women be structured?

Your observation on the patriarchal dimension of the traditional philosophy of friendship is striking. Why would friendship be fratriarchal? It is true that, more often than not, friends are conceived of as men among themselves, in their controlled and rational manliness, as colleagues and comrades. Fraternity – an equality of bodies, styles, culture and size – keeps others out. The archetypal depiction of the concord of male friends is in official or public dress, with all heads appearing on one level, in such a way that the signs of accord are all formal. Legitimate friends are rational citizens who agree on basic public issues: this is the liberalist construction that has dominated political discourse ever since the 1789 declaration of human rights.[4] This construction of political rationality is exclusive and I think that it appears in depictions of friendship too; while representations of male concord are inclusive and open to some extent, certain qualities seem to be required to be worthy a friend.

I suspect this may have something to do with the stabilising function of 'good affections'. Friendship seems to describe a connection undisturbed by desire, predominantly understood as a connection between mature subjects. It is, of course, affectionate, but these affections are, by definition, not threatening: friendship is an art of life, a form of the everyday. It is a confirmation of what we already are, rather than its interference.

In this sense friendship is reduced to a public agreement in line with liberal, contractual ideas. Should we understand it as a contract on agreed upon terms, or is it by definition in excess of any such rigid forms of agreement? 'In friendship and in politics', the German philosopher Hauke Brunkhorst writes, 'the citizens must, in a double sense, be free. They must find one another of their own free will, and they must be just as free from the cares of daily survival – thus, from labour – as they are from the will and commands of a master. Therefore, they can be neither slaves

3. See also Svetlana Boym, 'Scenography of Friendship', *Cabinet Magazine*, No. 36, winter 2009–10, pp. 88–94.

4. Ideal *citoyens* [citizens], as opposed to socially concrete *hommes* [men].

nor women. Only on the basis of manhood, affection, and property is a "complete", "good", and "self-sufficient life" possible.'[5]

Ancient tradition defines friendship as an exercise of freedom. And, as in most of the dominant examples throughout the history of philosophy, such a freedom is also defined negatively: freedom from mere affects and inclination, from the slavery of desires, etcetera. The condition of friendship is equality – which is why it excludes everyone who doesn't appear as such. In that tradition, women and slaves are not part of the construction of friendship, because they are not free and equal subjects, and are defined as affectionate beings, or dependent on labour. It is surprising how powerful these definitions still are in modern philosophy's history. Nietzsche aggressively states: 'Are you a slave? Then you cannot be a friend. Are you a tyrant? Then you cannot have friends. All-too-long have a slave and a tyrant been concealed in woman. Therefore woman is not yet capable of friendship: she knows only love.'[6]

Friendship, in this sense, needs to be exercised by and with free and equal subjects. However, only jurisdictional equality is what counts: if women and slaves are not considered part of the democratic space of the city, but just occupy the physical space of it, then friendship can only take place among men. Which also means that, according to this tradition, only free men can exercise freedoms like friendship. In a world in which women are subaltern, they cannot be addressed in friendship, and are therefore also excluded from its discourse. Hannah Arendt revives the polis model of freedom and places politics in the realm of action, and doesn't explicitly exclude slaves or women from the space of democracy, but neither does she include them. And she continues to disqualify what has traditionally been attributed to women and slaves: sensuousness and materiality.

I need to ask: what is the yet to be reached? And how about the friendship that women and slaves could have together and with each other? Could the idea of friendship among the excluded turn the problem on its head? Furthermore, could a woman speak in friendship?

5. Hauke Brunkhorst, *Solidarity. From Civic Friendship to a Global Legal Community,* MIT Press, 2005, p. 12.
6. Friedrich Nietzsche, *Thus Spoke Zarathustra*, translated by W. Kaufmann, Penguin, 1978 (1883–85), p. 57.

And in that way overcome the structure of classical philosophical discourse by occupying it, and acting within it?

If we were to engage in friendship in new terms, this could lead to what Arendt recalls in her friend Mary McCarthy: 'It's not that we think so much alike, but that we do this thinking-business for and with each other.'[(7)] *The 'thinking-business', I believe, is work in friendship, and friendship in work.*

But in this conception of 'thinking' and of 'sharing nothing but friendship alone' we have to be careful not to repeat a certain division of labour, a certain conception of the intellect that separates it in a self-sufficient way from material practices. In this sense, the gap between friendship and freedom on the one hand, and nature on the other, has always been a social differentiation. The price that is to be paid for the ethos of city life, the civilisation of the 'public happiness' of a ruling class, consists in the exclusion of the 'infamous people': the barbarians, foreigners, women, and slaves.[(8)]

There are questions about the possibility of friendship between men and women, but, of course, also between women or any other 'infamous people' themselves. Perhaps one way to proceed would be to think less of the whys of exclusion, and work on how to produce an inclusive discourse. How does friendship, as a relationship, takes place?

In Hannah Arendt's writing there is a concept of culture, which is close to what I would call friendship: she defines it as 'the company that one chooses to keep, in the present as well as in the past', quoting Cicero saying he'd rather go astray with Plato, than hold the truth with Pythagoras.[(9)] *What he means by this, I imagine, is that he prefers the company of Plato to a so-called truth, especially if proclaimed by a bore like Pythagoras; the politics of such a judgement are of a radical alliance. This is my interpretation of her redefinitions of culture, and the word friendship does not actually appear in her text, but 'the company one keeps' is neither the exclusive group of friends nor the production of life, but* cultura animi, *a kind of humanism. In this way the choices and*

7. Carol Brightman, ed., *Between Friends, The Correspondence of Hannah Arendt and Mary McCarthy, 1949–1975*, Harcourt Brace, 1995.
8. Brunkhorst, op. cit., p. 20.
9. Hannah Arendt, 'The Crisis in Culture: Its Social and Its Political Significance', *Between Past and Future: Eight exercises in political thought*, Faber and Faber, 1961, p. 226.

alliances that we make all the time (such as which books to read and refer to, or whom to work and think with), are instrumental in the formation of culture. I find this notion of friendship and/or culture quite empowering, perhaps even liberating, and was interested in not just understanding it in general, abstract terms, but through the specific situation of Arendt's friendship with McCarthy, taking place and speaking to me through twenty-five years of letters they exchanged, and the numerous books and publications they helped each other with.

If we speak about empowerment, let's also introduce Spinoza and his definition of friendship: for him friendship is an affectionate relationship in and through which humans mutually increase their *potentia agendi*, their vital capacities.

'To man, then, there is nothing more useful than man. Man, I say, can wish for nothing more helpful to the preservation of his being than that all should so agree in all things that the Minds and Bodies of all would compose, as it were, one Mind and one Body; that all should strive together, as far as they can, to preserve their being, and that all, together, should seek for themselves the common advantage of all' and: 'people bind themselves by those bonds most apt to make one people of them, and absolutely, to do those things which serve to strengthen friendships.'[10] There is potential in Spinoza to think friendship as something that goes beyond the restrictions of patriarchal reason and the abstractions of citizenship.[11] That also means that the rational citizen we mentioned is taken back into the materially concrete social existence of the human being. Such a form of connectedness transgresses the restrictions of friendship to rational concord, and can include those whose social existence is defined by material labour and intimate affections.

In other words, Spinoza sees friendship's highest potential as residing in the communal development of the intellect. I am particularly attracted to this view, as it emerges from refusing any ontological separation between mind and body. The formation of the common is, in this way, as much an agreement in terms of bodies as it is in terms of intellects, and the construction of a people is the construction of shared affects.

10. Spinoza, *Ethics*, l.c., *E*IVP18S and *E*IVApp XII.
11. Or rather, more appropriately *citoyenneté* [citizenship].

Michael Hardt, Antonio Negri and Paolo Virno have referred to these aspects of Spinoza's theory of society (a society grounded in the physical potentials to form solidarity and friendship). Here, friendship is no longer separated from labour, but rooted in 'affective labour', in the communal production of the common. And affective labour seems to have overcome the dismissal of affects in the name of nobility. In fact it echoes a long history of feminist discourse.

I would even say that friendship becomes a necessary moment of the political, as its constructive side. Virno writes: 'The characteristic of the "friend" is not merely that of sharing the same "enemy"; it is defined by the relations of solidarity that are established in the course of flight - by the necessity of working *together* to invent opportunities that up until that point have not been computed, and by the fact of their common participation in the Republic.'[12] Ultimately the question is: could friendship be a form of production? Could cooperation (as in service-oriented or industrial labour) also be a form of friendship? Could we conceive of the multitude in terms of an infinite friendship? Friendship could become a model of self-organisation, in which the autonomous production of our own lives is central. All this comes with the concept of cooperation, which has always been a leading concept for the socialist and communist movements. And in this sense the idea of the commune - a communality in production - and that of friendship are linked.

Friendship in this way leads towards the building of a common, the 'in common', or to a form of commoning. I went back to Aristotle, through Agamben's reading in the little book he published, The Friend, *and found something in it about desire: 'And as all people find the fact of their own existence desirable. The existence of their friends is equally - or almost equally - desirable. One must therefore also "consent" that his friend exists, and this happens by living together and by sharing acts and thoughts in common. In this sense, we say that humans live together, unlike cattle that share the pasture[...]'*[13]

What is the nature of this consent? How can we know about mutuality? Hegel, famously, both in line with and beyond Aristotle, discusses a dialectical

12. Paolo Virno, 'Virtuosity and Revolution: The Political Theory of Exodus', in Paolo Virno and Michael Hardt, eds., *Radical Thought in Italy A Potential Politics*, Minnesota University Press, 1996, pp.188-209, p. 204.
13. Giorgio Agamben, *The Friend*, Stanford University Press, 2009, p. 33.

moment in friendship: self-consciousness is an effect of mutual recognition (and this could be a conception of friendship). But how does one know that friendship is really mutual? How do we know that it is mutual when there are no formalised rules that can be taken as evidence for this consent? Hegel emphasises the dimension of struggle (for recognition), a continuous process of, on the one hand, overcoming the resistance in the self-will of the other, and on the other, the movement of trust, of letting go. Hence friendship is not just a relation but also a process (within which negativity is a driving moment – sublating [aufheben] all the necessary struggle, fear, and mistrust).

This would indeed suggest that desire plays a part in friendship, but at one level removed: not as wanting something from the other. Friendship in these terms cannot be based simply on utility or pleasure, but as a desire for the other to exist, as a desire for life, and for cohabitation within it. This is the idea of living together and sharing acts and thoughts in common, so that what is shared is not property, things, objects, or even qualities (being this or that, including siblings, artists, or French) but an activity, a process of co-existence through doing and thinking. Which brings me back to Arendt, for isn't that what she calls 'words and deeds'?

Furthermore, the activity of spending time with things, that I consider part of the process of making work, allows other forms of friendship not dependent on reciprocity to exist – by way of which I can befriend Arendt's thinking, and work with it.

But maybe something more than arguments need to be shared with a true friend. And there may be no strictly rational, argumentative reasons for friendship, which problematises whether we need words for it. Don't friends understand each other without words? Being friends might be a form of affectionate consent (sensed, felt, habitually agreed upon) rather than an intellectual agreement.

What kind of action and or consent does this propose? The reasons to love someone are valid only when we do already love this person. That thought is abysmal: you can never produce reasons to be amicably loved. Friendship would be built upon grace – the grace of being liked.

While to be chosen as the recipient of friendship might feel like being touched by grace, it is no grace to engage in being a friend; here we are responsible for our choices and actions.

These were the unconditional elements in friendship, and we can now ask whether it is characteristic of autonomous human beings. And if so, whether the idea of autonomy is far more deeply rooted in sensuousness, affection and materiality than we might have thought.

There are, however, also enabling powers to friendship. What is the potential of doing something in friendship? There is an emancipatory dimension to choosing one's allies, committing to issues and deciding to take them on, which can be a force that propels us forward. I think there is a collective aspect to this empowerment, which is the congruence between friendship and solidarity: the knowledge of engaging in a common project, of contributing to building the world, which is also how friendship leads to politics. This of course is also a drive to self-organisation.

This line of thought might avoid us the political pitfalls of a patriarchal construction of public reasoning. But the question of the discourse of friendship's patriarchal construction instigates another one: even if friendship is grounded in sameness, must it necessarily be exclusive? While friendship is part of a narrative of the particular, it sometimes claims to be the true form of the universal. Adorno writes: 'Indiscriminate benevolence towards all constantly threatens that coldness and remoteness against each, which are once again communicated to the whole.' If so, the 'injustice of friendship' 'is the medium of true justice.'[14] Can the particularist, partialist perspective of friendship be reconciled with universalist claims? Or, put simpler, is friendship only about the respective us, or is it, to some extent, about all of us, too?

Perhaps friendship is less about doing something together, constantly addressing each other, and more about enabling each to be oneself, allowing each other for the silence of not taking part. Friendship might be about shared loneliness rather than overly explicit togetherness. Is the connectivity in such loneliness structurally invisible? Solidarity and thus, a certain dimension of friendship, might have something to

14. Theodor W. Adorno, *Minima Moralia. Reflexions From Damaged Life*, translated by E.F.N. Jephcott, Verso, 1974 (1951), p. 77.

do with mutual support in situations of lack and need. We might be friends as we share nothingness – like August Sander's photographs of blind children seem to do. If there is a politics of friendship that would enable that, it would have to reject the idea of sensuous plenitude.

In this sense solitude appears to be dialectical: aren't we friends precisely as we acknowledge each other's solitude?[15] Isn't modernity in that sense a condition of friendship, too? We are never immediately and authentically friends. Friendship could in fact be conceived of as the reflection of a lost authenticity. That is the greatly modern trait of friendship.

I would support the necessity of a certain estrangement, beyond lack or need: it seems important that friendship should come in excess of, perhaps rather than as opposed to, lack and deficiency. Being a friend might and should entail, I believe, helping out, however, it is always more than that. Solitude is, nevertheless, not the term I would choose, and I am doubtful at best of the accuracy or even possibility of being oneself – and I know I am the sum of what I have read, heard, spoken and experienced. It is essential to behold an unknown dimension in and for our friends, and a reciprocal estrangement, on the basis on which we can be friends.

'Friendship, this relation without dependence, without episode, yet into which all of the simplicity of life enters, passes by the way of the recognition of the common strangeness that does not allow us to speak of our friends but only to speak to them, [...] the movement of understanding in which, speaking to us, they reserve, even on the most familiar terms, an infinite distance, the fundamental separation on the basis of which what separates becomes relation.'[16] If this is the form of friendship we have been looking for, then its potential is both revealed and obscured by Blanchot's sentence, in the condition that if we cannot speak of our friends then we perhaps cannot even speak of friendship. We however can and do speak to our friends, which is already to act in friendship, as a practice, a process.

Friendship in this form becomes productive and cooperative, a pragmatic form of subjects organising themselves. Friendship is able to manifest

15. Hannah Arendt's distinction between loneliness and solitude is fruitful here, see also Svetlana Boym, op.cit.
16. Maurice Blanchot, *Friendship*, Stanford University Press, 1997, p. 291.

collective autonomy beyond lack or need, and beyond the plenitude of sameness. While we have to end this conversation here, we could do that by proposing friendship as an elective affinity without finality.[17]

17. As it was beautifully put by Svetlana Boym, op. cit., p. 93.

THE ALMOST INSTITUTION

Livia Pancu

Eight artists initiated the contemporary art organisation Vector in 2001.[1] Being a fine art student in Iași at the time, I first started to work for Vector in 2003, and I became its director in June 2011, until May 2012, when I resigned to join tranzit.ro,[2] which is part of a transnational network of cultural institutions.[3] Looking back at the development of Vector, it is clear that it started out with shared authorship, where our work was characterised by experiment, dedication, and self-organisation. We developed new knowledge and new social spaces in our city, but that came accompanied with exhaustion caused by our dis-organisation. The gradual maturing of those involved made us embark on a process of transformation: from a group of invested professionals towards an institutional format. Or at least that is what we thought we were doing, but whether the institutional format was a real aim or something created out of a particular necessity and desire in our context remains to be determined.

'Becoming an Institution' and 'Being the Almost Institution' are two notions that sit at the centre of my reflections upon Vector today. The first includes a transformative process towards what I presume Vector's members understood it as, being an institution within the specific context of Iași. The latter describes a potentially static position that sums up the yet unfulfilled desires and projections of the same group of people on an image of the institution. Despite the fact that the becoming was embraced as a working method of our group, the almost seems to better encapsulate the way we actually functioned.

Since Vector's legal status was that of an association, it was an entity constituted and run by partners with equal powers and duties. This was the principle we tried to follow, although in reality we were actively heading towards an abstract structure characterised by hierarchy, a set of rules and practices, stability, archiving and institutional memory as well as continuity, all of which fulfilling the image of the institution for contemporary art that we could build in Iași. The 'Almost' was created by the intersection between the equity partners' visions, which in turn overlapped with a hierarchical way of working among us. This tension kept Vector somewhere in the middle, while transforming and becoming

1. Dan Acostioaei, Dragoş Alexandrescu, Matei Bejenaru, Felix Drăgan, Cezar Lăzărescu, Florin Grigoraş, Mihai Voicu and Bogdan Teodorescu, all artists. In 2005 five other members with various backgrounds joined: Alexandru Bounegru, Genţiana Baciu, Cătălin Gheorghe, Vlad Morariu, Livia Pancu and Iulia Tencariu.
2. See http://ro.tranzit.org/en.
3. See http://www.tranzit.org/.

were a permanent condition. More than ten years since its inception, Vector and its members found themselves at a crossroads needing to decide how to continue.

Iași is a city in eastern Romania. Our closest peers are in Bucharest, which is 406 km away, in Cluj, 390 km away, and Chisinău, in the Republic of Moldova, 180 km away. Before Vector was established, no contemporary art institution with connections to an international art network existed in the region. The motivations for initiating Vector included a certain sense of responsibility towards the local context.

For those running Vector it was essential to facilitate the production of art that connected with the international scene and with large-scale exhibitions, as a means to create and educate an audience. Throughout the years a big institutional infrastructure was simulated by organising a wide variety of projects, including an international biennial, the long term socio-cultural project cARTier, running a gallery space and a residency programme, as well as publishing magazines and books.[4] The complexities of these projects unavoidably led to a discussion on the potential of overproduction. All our projects provided means for self-education, both for the public as well as for ourselves. However, these situations also expressed Vector's ambitions to become an institution for contemporary art in dialogue with discussions happening elsewhere.

Our knowledge of contemporary art came from a rather limited network of artists and curators to begin with, based on our personal networks and contacts, and our projects were supported by a handful of funding structures and organisations that had specific demands on our activities. Today we still see elements that are remnants of the curators and art institutions that worked with Vector throughout its first years. The disadvantage of this was that we behaved in a mimetic manner, trying to follow and apply models that came from somewhere else. However, the most important role in projecting the ambitions of a big institution wanting to contextualise its activity and its interest in creating a legacy was played by Vector members themselves. All our programmes

4. Vector's history is intertwined with the history of the Periferic Festival and Biennial, the first biennial in Romania, which was initiated by Vector's co-founder Matei Beienaru (1997–2008). Vector was the organiser of cARTier project (2004–07), Vector Gallery (2004–07) and partner in the Backyard Residency (2006–07) and Accented Residency (2009–10) programmes, and published *Vector* magazine and *Vector – critical research in context*. Currently Vector's activities are invisible and more focused on positioning itself in its own history as well as in the surrounding society, apart from its participation in the ENPAP project (European Network for Public Art Producers) (2010–12).

reflected and simulated an institution, and formed the strategy we chose to articulate ourselves within the local and the international artistic contexts. I would, however, claim that what we did was rather embody the Almost Institution.

We wished to create a stable organisation that could transcend the individuals that had formed it, and the use of the term institution was somehow inflicted upon us. Our legal status as an association sat us closer to the self-organised format, rather than that of the institutional. We often described ourselves as 'a group of people', while our behaviour could periodically be characterised by strict rules and hierarchy.

When this discrepancy was occurring, we were actively discussing the institutionalisation of Vector. It was necessary to present the organisational structure as sustainable, which would benefit the dialogue with potential funding bodies, where use of the right terminology was instrumental in securing financial support. Within the organisation we thought that the Almost Institution could offer this image more strongly than that of the artist-run organisation. Although this image only remained a simulated projection, as we never allowed ourselves to become personally detached from Vector, and the knowledge we gradually developed over time stayed within our own group.

Another external pressure was constituted by the fact that when Vector was initiated there was no museum or other kind of national institution focused on contemporary art in Romania. Vector and other active organisations were therefore acting as substitutes, and were taking responsibility for critical discourse across the country. The National Museum of Contemporary Art was only inaugurated in 2004 in Bucharest. Soon after, the activities of this museum became almost irrelevant for part of the Romanian contemporary art scene, or part of the scene became irrelevant for the museum, which is why existing organisations across the country kept their roles and positions.

Because of the lack of strong institutions, and the need for production platforms for contemporary art, Vector had to present itself, adapt and act in many different ways, matching the type of projects we were running. At the time we could not see this as being flexible, since we were always changing. Thus, the only way we could characterise ourselves was through a promise: the promise of institutionalisation. We ended up using self-organisation as the only possible method to evolve and transform towards the institution, a stable model.

Vector members dreamt about this transformation for different reasons. The initial group consisted of eight artists who by 2006 had different motivations for still being involved. Nevertheless, their main drive was the possibility to produce their own work, exhibit, and get critical feedback from art professionals. Therefore their role in Vector transgressed from being organisers who occasionally would take part in exhibitions that they produced into being artists represented through Vector's activities. For the initial group Vector's institutionalisation was introduced out of the necessity as formulated by the new members, who slowly took over the organisers' role. By that time Vector was already over-producing. We had to deal with a huge amount of work,[5] which required at least ten people,[6] who were all gradually learning along the way. In retrospect it is clear that this made us focus solely on the realisation of projects and did not allow any room for reflection on the contents and the direction things were taking. We were merely trying to stay afloat.

By the end of the 2008 Periferic Biennial, the last biennial to date, Vector's members and close collaborators were exhausted and lacked the motivation to continue. Many of them had second jobs to earn a living, others went abroad to study, and the rest wanted to focus on their own artistic careers. Many of the relations between the individuals in the group were eroded and there was a lack of energy needed to work towards getting new members. In 2010 co-founder and director Matei Bejenaru decided to let go of Vector. He organised a conference with former collaborators (artists, curators and representatives of other institutions) to debate the future of Vector and later that year we published a small book on Vector's activities 1997–2010.

With the support of the former director I decided to use this moment to change the strategy of Vector. Instead of working in our own geographical context, where we had been active for ten years, we accepted every international invitation to collaborate abroad. This allowed us to focus strategies needed to present Vector elsewhere and formulate notions of the kind of work we had done to date. Vector's year

5. In 2005-2006 Vector was responsible for the Periferic 7 (three sections with four curators), the cARTier Project, the Vector Gallery with exhibitions every three weeks, the residency programmes, publications, the website as well as the visual identity for all the projects, layout and proofing for all the publications, application writing, budgeting, etc.

6. Dan Acostioaei, Dragoş Alexandrescu, Matei Bejenaru, Cătălin Gheorghe, Andrei Gavril (finance), Vlad Morariu, Cristian Nae (on a specific section of the biennial in 2006), Livia Pancu, Iulia Tencariu and Bogdan Teodorescu.

on the road became a turning point which constituted a moment for much needed contemplation and reflection, and came at the precise time when most of us realised the degree of disconnection we were facing between each other.(7) My attempt to run Vector in a very horizontal manner was due to fail because it could not be applied realistically within our group. What I had inherited was a great portfolio from an organisation that had been active until 2008, but that was exhausted. The dramatic differences in our expectations of what Vector was and should be had simply grown too big, and it seemed impossible at this point to engage with an audience, when we couldn't even find a common ground to work from among ourselves. We might have been able to go on simulating a while longer, but I'm not sure we would have been able to maintain respect for each other. Instead, by the end of 2011 artist Florin Bobu and I proposed to pause our programming and push all of us to focus on Vector as a group.(8)

As a consequence of ceasing the programme Vector became invisible to everyone outside the group.(9) The simple decision that rendered Vector invisible was not easy to make, since we had to step back from projects that we had already committed to.(10) The pressure from the outside had been growing, but in a way this also helped us reach this radical decision and to implement it immediately. However, the question remained how to communicate this decision to our audience and peers. Do you start being invisible by making a very visible public statement and transforming this into a new strategy of appearance?

For many, the fact that Vector was not doing what it had previously done, could mean that it was dead, or that it was falling prey to a slow death. If the process of becoming invisible is not declared publicly and

7. The phrase *'Vector's year on the road'* came about in a discussion with curator Jesse McKee. It included the following: participation in the Frame section of the Frieze Art Fair in London in October 2010; an exhibition project at Western Front in Vancouver in February 2011; participation in the Vienna Art Fair in May 2011; and participation in Preview Berlin Art Fair in September 2011 (the latest included a separate faction of Vector: studio for art practices and debates).
I must also mention that during this time a core group took over, formed by three previous active members, two founding members who had more or less stepped back in recent years, and two collaborators.

8. Florin Bobu is an artist based in Iași and the only (invisible) active Vector collaborator who specifically spent time and ideas on what the new Vector could be. At his wish, he is not a Vector member.

9. This decision was also influenced by a very productive meeting with ENPAP fellows, a closed and confidential one, during which we had to expose ourselves as an organisation and receive critical feedback.

10. Florin Bobu came up with this formulation in one of our intense dialogues. See also *Faculty of Invisibility Project* initiated by Inga Zimprich, department of Learning, tutor Nebojsa Milikic.

explained there is a danger for these interpretations to start circulating. Another danger seemed to be that it seemed we did not know which future we were heading towards. As with a biennial, the only time for invisibility is when preparing for the announcement of a new curator and preparing the concept of the next edition. Similarly for Vector the future had to look bright in order for this period of invisibility to be acceptable within its national and international networks. It is important to note that this text could be interpreted as the first sign of visibility for Vector since I was its director, but I would like to state that since I am writing in retrospect from a very personal perspective, these views might not be shared entirely by my colleagues.

Vector was now working very slowly on its mechanics and we were trying to fight the desire to produce and allow this state to gradually take its own course. The stakes were high, but the benefits were equally as promising: the former image of Vector was transforming and slowly disappearing, which could potentially allow for a situation in which we would feel less inclined to work with projects created by inertia and instead be inspired by the reality surrounding us.

Of course, the image of the institution that we had projected so easily earlier was still haunting us. The image was something we all believed in and something we held on to, as it was necessary for our sense of belonging to the professional art world. Throughout the years of Vector's existence, only during three of them we were in a somewhat stable situation, which allowed us to run a gallery programme.[11] What we knew was that the biennial, the publication of magazines, and running a gallery space are activities that need a stable platform with a proper infrastructure to operate in a sustainable manner. The symbolic investment of all the people involved in projects over the years was compensated for by a shared dream of stability, which would eventually allow complete freedom to work, which was a utopia based on false premises. Stability meant first of all a singular vision in order to have a high degree of flexibility in approaching funding bodies. For stability to happen we needed a clear institutional vision to be shared by all members. Given the different visions among Vector's membership it is hard to imagine a situation in which no one would feel the need to compromise.

11. The singular period when Vector came closest to the image of a stable format of an institution was between 2004 and 2007, when the cARTier project took place.

What I am not able to answer is the question what Vector will become when it remerges. Previously it had always been about surviving and letting the models and idiosyncrasies inherited from the past live on, and letting the multiple agendas of the different individuals forming Vector run in parallel to the overall ambitions. After ten years Vector has remained a curiosity, even for local art professional, often described as putting on 'unconventional' exhibitions.

The notion of a directorship and a horizontal structure do not go well together. As a result a last solution came to me: to really perform the role of the director, which was even harder within the given conditions. Dreaming of the previous more horizontal formats of Vector was not productive, but I hoped we would nevertheless be able to act together as a group. What I imagined for Vector was to be actively aware and engaged with the fast-changing Romanian society, encourage collaborations with local and regional institutions, thus creating a real dialogue, while always being aware of what simulation in these circumstances can bring. The further development of Vector is, however, not my call anymore.

From May 2012 a new management and artistic team have been put in place. The new group will find new ways of developing both the organisation and the flow of individual energies, and I hope they will use the past year of invisibility to re-consider what activities are needed, and from there regenerate Vector. The invisibility should be seen as a brutal, but necessary, link in the chain of events in Vector's life, as an activity just as important as any other. Without previously having tested invisibility as an exercise, it was a sensitive activity to engage in. Sometimes it seemed to help the flow of ideas and sometimes we got stuck, mainly because of our separate agendas. Eventually the self-induced invisibility led to my departure, but hopefully also to the ideological coagulation of the people that have decided to take over.

Internationally, we created ourselves as a periphery, but at the same time we also created a centre to refer to. However, we ignored the fact we allegedly also took on the role of a centre for other peripheries.[12] According to the Vector model that I have tried to describe above, I dare say that the lessons learnt are that the periphery has to act with caution and that invisibility can also be a form of existence!

12. This idea was very much discussed by Florin Bobu, whose work was partly realised in Tecuci, his native city. Tecuci is an old city at the intersection of historical commercial routes, which currently has 40,000 inhabitants and is halfway between Iași and Bucharest.

82 – 91

WHAT HAPPENED, HAPPENED

Linus Elmes

(1)

Geographically speaking, it began at bar El Mundo at Erstagatan 21, Södermalm, Stockholm, Sweden. It was on the first of May 2006 that I declared an inconspicuous cubbyhole an art space and myself its director. The space itself was 3.75 metre square and located in an awkward room between the bar and the restroom. The bar's owners, Björn and Kristina Sjöö, had asked me if I could do something, like an artistic take on that difficult space. The implied question was whether I could paint something decorative on the wall. When instead – impulsively, but in all seriousness – I suggested starting an art space they reacted in a very positive way.

They put the room at my disposal and guaranteed me artistic freedom and self-determination. Ersta Konsthall would have its own agenda, distinctly separate from that of the bar. At the same time, the bar's owners agreed to finance its activities. This included a nominal monthly salary, production costs, and remuneration for the artists in the shape of a three-course dinner, including drinks. It was all sealed in a contract.

(2)

The idea was to start a sort of self-reflexive art space that would evaluate and review institutional conditions.

(3)

Initially, I was interested in what kinds of mechanisms constitute an institution, and imagined the art space as both an operative instrument and an exploratory experiment. What kinds of values are produced in an institution, and how do these values relate to society at large? The art space was not to be an exemplary model, but a working one. The point was to create a manageable format in which I could produce every exhibition myself and thereby oversee the sources and forms of funding, the means of production, communication, channels of distribution and forms of transmission.

I didn't understand this at the time, but in retrospect the first projects of the art space appeared like a suggestion towards the possibility of a different order of things. This included a number of rather basic assertions, such as: this too can be an art space; this too is a way to finance one's operations; I too can be the director of an art space.

The goal was not to critique or problematise. I didn't want to establish an artists' initiative, and neither did I want to be an *alternative* to one thing or a *copy* of something else. I simply didn't like the idea that something would be formed through consensus. I knew why I started the art space and my ambition was to formulate myself around that, and to be as clear about my own agenda as possible.

(4)

My own experience, combined with conversations with other artists working in self-financed, artist-run initiatives proved that it was possible to create organisations true to the principles and goals of the endeavour. Methods often applied were, of course, direct democracy, or 'flat' structures, that made the independent initiative come across as much more utopian, and maybe even modern and innovative, than the large, slow-moving and hierarchically structured art institutions.

At the same time, large, general shortcomings in some of the artists' initiatives can be identified. Often they are forced to accept temporary, short-term solutions, as they face difficulties locating funds, especially the kind of long-term support that can grant security and continuity, often due to administrative inexperience. And insecurity is, as we know, time-consuming. These factors position the artists' initiative, consciously or unconsciously, as 'alternative'.

(5)

I wanted Ersta Konsthall to be a fully functional institutional machine in motion, like a hands-on pragmatic model for simulation of institutional activity. Different from other artist-run experiments, I had funding that was linked to the context at hand. My financial independence made it possible to avoid the most obvious pitfalls, and as a result I escaped being categorised all too definitively.

Ersta Konsthall was never anything physical, not even when it had a physical location. It was more a materialised idea: it became what I said it was. In essence, it was both a work and an artistic strategy.

This brought a lot of advantages compared to other organisational forms. Firstly, I didn't need to be commercial, represent artists or sell art.

Secondly, I could avoid institutional demands like commissions, public goals, and dependence on external funding. Additionally, I escaped the third alternative: of having members who pay a fee or contribute a varying number of working hours in order, paradoxically, to run an endeavour founded on one's own commitment to it. That becomes a vicious circle: funding something in order to be able to continue funding it, as if that in itself were the purpose. After all, I had asserted that the minuscule site at hand was an art space and that I was its director, and, therefore, so I was. For me it was like writing a story. I had room to focus on what, for lack of a better word, might be called the manuscript.

I set about creating various thought figures. As much as Ersta Konsthall was a reaction against working with exhibition production as a collective process, it was also an exploration of various other levels of collaboration. Ersta Konsthall as a thought figure emanated from my person, out towards its surroundings, preconditions and possibilities. The art space treated ritualised institutional behavioural patterns, illuminating these patterns and structures by appropriating them and displacing their meaning.

I read the mission statements of various institutions, and studied and imitated their structures. Larger museums and art spaces are conglomerates: I always kept this in mind while communicating about or profiling Ersta Konsthall, even if I never spelled it out. But in order to tell the story of what I did as Ersta Konsthall, I imagined that there were a number of different functions: a programme committee, super-intendants and curators, heads of personnel and sponsorship, as well as press secretaries, heads of information, technicians, event coordinators, and archivists. I began actively proclaiming the agenda of the art space in my press releases. Working on programming and communications I created an institutional establishment, partly imaginary and partly functional. Ersta Konsthall was neither big nor small, but both. Ersta Konsthall was an experiment in miniature and a working institution.

(6)

As a result of all this Ersta Konsthall gained a position in the world. By working on and evaluating its activities in relation to the larger social game, and through a self-reflexive approach, I added narrative elements to the structure. The art space became highly visible. In terms of attention and the creation of a profile, it was very successful. Within a short amount of time the art space between a bar and its restrooms appeared to be an established art institution.

The radio and entertainment sections caught on and told the story of this miniature art space, even the small-town papers reviewed and wrote about it. Its size had an obvious news value, and I was often asked whether the space was 'Sweden's smallest' or even 'the world's smallest'. Initially, I avoided the subject, because I saw the risk of superficiality with regards to the project. Later on, I used it to describe physical size as something irrelevant, pointing instead at the deeds and the doing, which exceeded the spatial limits of the room. Additionally, I knew that the size in itself was not unique. There are many examples of other tiny exhibition spaces, including Maurizio Cattelan, Massimiliano Gioni and Ali Subotnick's The Wrong Gallery, Modern Talking's Minigalleriet, and Jacob Fabricius's KBH Kunsthal.

(7)

Four months after the conception of the art space - two months earlier than planned - the bar's owners and I evaluated the project together. We concluded that the frequency of visitors to the art space had had a positive effect on sales for the bar. The increase in the number of visitors simply spilled over into their till. The opening night crowds were largest early on, when the place still had news value; later on there was a slight oscillation on that front, but numbers were never bad. Of course, 600 to 700 people in a bar with a capacity of 150 led to a certain buzz, which generated visitors during the exhibition periods as well. Perhaps it was logical. The inverse relationship was fantastic. If customers who'd come to the bar for a glass or two wanted to use the bathroom, they would be forced to pay a visit to the art space. The bar was open six days a week. No one actually kept count, but 2-3,000 visitors a month made Ersta Konsthall one of the most frequently visited art institutions in Stockholm. We concluded the evaluation by extending the contract for a year.

(8)

One aspect of running an art space located in a bar was that the act of contemplating art was severely de-dramatised. There was no unspoken barrier demanding insidership, group belonging or social codes. In this sense, Ersta Konsthall was very successful already during the period at Erstagatan, one of its goals being the democratisation of the distribution of art and attracting new types of visitors. It was a felicitous interaction with the outside world: a bar and an art space in harmony with one another.

Another observation I made concerned the optimal relationship in size between the bar and the art space. The relationship at Ersta Konsthall between the size of the exhibition space and the space devoted to social activity was ideal. When I pictured the bar as a part of the art space and not the other way around, I felt like I was discovering a more honest architecture.

At the turn of 2006 to 2007, I invited Amelie Rydqvist to do a project entitled *Konsthall*. *Konsthall* was an animated film in which a three-dimensional model of the art space flies like an airborne vessel, and, in a shower of sparks, docks with the restroom. This also entailed an actual rebuilding of the art space, including integrating the restroom into the space through expanding its territory at the expense of the bar.

For me, Amelie's project dealt with a couple of fundamental issues. The room, which previously had undergone a rather drastic change in character, and continued to transform with each exhibition, was now a white cube, thus presenting a clearer picture of the art space as a system.

The project meant a turning point: for the first time I realised that the art space in many respects was larger than the bar. It was a question of attitude, but it also had to do with the fact that the programme and presence of the art space was chiselled more clearly into the collective mind of the visitors. The majority said that they were going to Ersta Konsthall, not to El Mundo. This indicated a hierarchical relationship, in which the art space was positioned above the bar. The bar's owners, Björn and Kristina, were quick to repossess the bathroom as soon as Amelie's project ended, by painting it pink and placing a large flamingo on one wall and coloured lights over the sink. However, the power balance had shifted irrevocably.

(9)

Elin Wikström did the next exhibition, and she proposed a project that was conceived to attract bar guests. In response to the flamingo on the wall, I announced her project as the first in which the art space with its limited resources had come up with a pragmatic solution and that stretched beyond the boundaries of the room. It was a comment on the relationships between architectural territories and the projects' physical situation and accommodation within the bar.

At the opening, Elin introduced the project and let the visitors become familiar with the work and its participants: what she launched was a Pub Quiz. On wet Wednesdays during the exhibition period, three-person teams, consisting of invited representatives of Stockholm's art scene, competed against each other, measuring their skills and knowledge of conceptual and context-based art. Regular guests were free to form their own teams to challenge these authorities. Elin and I developed the questions together and took turns at being quizmaster.

Almost a year had passed, and for me it felt like it was time to change the circumstances of the art space. More and more often, I was invited to participate in different contexts and I could no longer keep up my commitment. The question as to whether claiming to be an artistic director was enough to actually become one 'for real', had also been answered and the art space partially had its own life. The next question concerned the extent to which the art space was connected to my person. If Ersta Konsthall in fact was a format, the identity of its director shouldn't matter so much.

I planned to look for a replacement but I abandoned the thought of a direct transferral of my role. Instead, I engaged two recently graduated curators, Paola Zamora and Sofia Curman. I gave them my small salary to share. But I also stayed on to take care of strategy, communications and profiling. In practice, the workload remained more or less the same, but I had more flexibility in relation to the use of my time, and I wasn't bound to administrative duties in the same way.

(10)

One immediate change that came about when Paola and Sofia started working at the art space, was the way in which the exhibitions were chosen and produced. The most important and decisive difference was that they related more to the art space as an exhibition space than I ever had. For me, the *idea* of Ersta Konsthall has always been the primary issue: that it was a room located where it was was a secondary matter to me. It might as well have been a box in the woods or a storefront: every imaginable space would have had to subject itself to the idea. Sofia and Paola were of course more predisposed to seeing Ersta Konsthall as an established concept. To them it was an exhibition space, albeit a small one – but still, a space.

They invited Swedish artist Tova Mozard for their first exhibition, and it became clear that it was a 'real exhibition', with a framed photo on one wall and a video on the other. There wasn't really anything in the conveying of the work itself that differed from my own practice. It wasn't about the hanging, presentation or choice of artist, it was a matter of approach and attitude. There was something resolved, something that hadn't been there with me. Simply put, they had a relationship to the room rather than the idea.

Their work brought about the institutionalisation of the art space, which was good, because it became obvious that the idea was so clearly profiled and so crystallised that through an external process it finally had materialised as its own mimetic copy. This made me understand even more clearly how perceptions are constructed and fabricated. But it also meant that the art space risked becoming fixed as something wholly dependent on the premises at Erstagatan.

In light of this, it became more obvious to me that the gesture, the fact of working with two curators, was the central thing. That was more important than the actual exhibitions they produced. What happened in the space was to me less significant.

(11)

An unforeseeable effect of our increased institutionalisation was that Björn and Katarina finally started to feel they were feeding a monster. I started to consider the alternatives. In a way this was liberating.

I realised that since I was in charge of communications regarding the programme of the space, I had the power. Since I didn't consider the art space to be dependent on the space as such, there was no point entering into a polemic.

(12)

I circulated a message describing the situation in the following way:

> Starting on 5 August 2007, Ersta Konsthall will operate in a nomadic format. The practice of Ersta Konsthall will be reassessed, geographically as well as with regards to frequency, in the months to come.

On different occasions and over different periods of time, Ersta Konsthall will, in various ways and with varying levels of participation, materialise in diverse places.

(13)

After circulating the message about the new nomadic existence of the art space, we were offered a number of different engagements at different sites.

I was sceptical of the intentions behind some of the invitations, and suspected that Ersta Konsthall would work as an alibi for those. The inviting parties knew what they wanted and were going to make use of the synergetic effects of doing it in collaboration with Ersta Konsthall. Meanwhile, the offer could be wrapped in terms like, 'the longstanding commitment of the museum towards the integration of contemporary art and older art in the museum's collections.' In part, it became abundantly clear what a flexible art institution Ersta Konsthall really was. In relation to other institutions' slow-moving administrative structure, this became apparent in an almost pedagogical manner. And in part, I was more convinced than ever that I was the one who decided what Ersta Konsthall was and what it did. My interest lay in inter-institutional collaboration, and our different agendas and working conditions were part and parcel of that.

One easily becomes devoured by something that is larger than oneself. Sofia and Paola, who took care of daily communications, made great concessions and several times they wanted to give up. It was obvious to me: the institution needed us, but we didn't need it.

Through that second circulation, several important elements of the future fell into place: about the preconditions of the narrative in the practice, and about communication as an instrument for developing and positioning a project's identity by formulating an agenda and remaining faithful to it.

Ersta Konsthall had begun as a site-specific experiment, then evolved into a nomadic state, but it was by now ready for another form of existence where its embodied qualities was taken to its logical end. My own apprehension of Ersta Konsthall – if there was any – was about the possibilities of constructing any given identity within a larger structure. It's the kind of absolute freedom that allows you to write your own history.

This knowledge led inevitably to the final dissolution of Ersta Konsthall. There was no reason to hold on to the physical aspects of an imaginary construction.

92 - 101

MY HISTORY OF THE HISTORY OF L'APPARTEMENT 22

Abdellah Karroum

This text is composed by several experiences and proposals that could have been successive chapters. However, I am taking the risk of writing and presenting them interwoven and intersecting, creating a structure of potential conflict. Firstly, there is the history of an art space, which is available and shared through public programmes and publications. Secondly, there are calls to create more independent spaces and to assert their methodologies, and this history could contribute to that process. And thirdly, I introduce the idea of rupture to position art in a larger political landscape to voice a resistance to the general 'facebookisation' of intellectual activities.

The narrative of L'appartement 22 as an independent space in Morocco is transformed by its own actions. Carving out a locally engaged artistic direction, as well as observing international ones, is a survival strategy. Not so much a strategy for the particular physical space, but for the survival of freedom to organise such work. This is therefore a reflection not only on L'appartement 22, but also on other independent spaces. The narrative I have created can be seen as part of a history of independent art spaces on the African continent (and elsewhere), since the African continent's most progressive art scene is primarily developed by independent initiatives. But here we have to bear in mind that independent initiative does not only take place outside of institutions, but also within them, and that initiatives inside institutions are as commendable as those in totally new spaces. But, what applies to all of them is that the parameters of 'freedom' are guaranteed through real changes, not through listing articles in a written constitution.

Projects led by the spaces that are the most resistant to circumstantial, regionalist, communal, speculative or populist developments are those that work closest with artists that engages with the surrounding society, and follow the implications of their artworks. These are acts of resistance in the search for a vocabulary connected to society, rather than to the platforms and networks in which capital is invested, where the meaning of the works is no more than their market value. These are places that unfold around their contents, not out of a priori created containers. Artist Frédéric Bruly Bouabré's 'temple' in the suburb of Abidjan in the Ivory Coast, is one such space: a blackboard hangs on the outside wall of his family home, transforming the street into a 'classroom' where to teach his invented artistic vocabulary. It creates a space for instruction and meetings, and becomes a reference point to the everydayness of an entire community. This blackboard opens onto the world, onto oral histories and the history of writing.

Another example can be a street in Dakar, which transformed into an art space for a few days in 2012 by a collective intervention from artists who organised exchanges with the neighbourhood youth around questions of noise and expression. A garage was transformed into a site of production through meetings, mural experiments and recorded discussions on hip-hop poetry, and the street became a space for open expression.(1) These are actions that take place every day around the world and these are 'formactive' collaborations that largely act in spaces that take on the form of what happens there.(2)

The creation of independent spaces, following specific ideas and dreams, is a strategy used in a number of urban contexts, but also beyond, in socio-cultural contexts in which official programmes cannot - or do not want to - respond to the necessity of bringing citizens together to realise the 'social idea'.(3) I would claim that the emergence of physical spaces, as well as editorial spaces, where ideas about artistic and curatorial practices are shared, are appropriate responses to the necessity of producing platforms and places for encounters and debates. Taking Morocco as an example, and the example of L'appartement 22 in particular: we are aware of the experimental possibilities and limits that confront this project. This annotated reprisal of L'appartement 22's history is a chance to re-situate this specific project space as a unique experiment and to re-position it in a larger context.

The story that introduces the book that documents L'appartement 22's first six years begins like this:(4)

'Ten October 2002 is a Thursday like any other in Rabat. The cries of the educated and unemployed [Diplômés chômeurs] dominate the aural landscape on the Avenue Mohamed V. I have been living here for five months already! Safaa and Younès are finishing the installation of *Brisa* and *Cafane* after sharing the residency in my apartment for two weeks. Tonight,

1. During Gabriella Ciancimino's residency in Dakar, Ciancimino was invited by L'appartement 22. See the video on Radio Apartment 22 (R22): www.radioapartment22.com.
2. The term 'Formactive' links 'form', from the artistic vocabulary, and 'action' into an adjective for the engaged artwork.
3. A term proposed on R22 by Juan Gaitàn and Abdellah Karroum for a discussion among L'appartement 22's Curatorial Delegation.
4. The following are extracts of 'My History of L'appartement 22 (2002-2008)', which was published in the book *L'appartement 22 2002-2008*, ed. Abdellah Karroum, éditions hors'champs, 2009.

the first exhibition opens, *JF_JH (Individualités)*,[5] a camera frames the view from the window and the lively image of the street is projected in the exhibition space. Clearly, it's the beginning of something...

L'appartement 22 exists because of what takes form there and what lives there. The artworks born at L'appartement 22 have transformed this home into an art space. They have given it the sense of this exigency, this ethic of production. Over the years, the space has become an amphitheatre, a museum gallery, and a place for meetings and events about art.

L'appartement 22's events have definitively changed the artistic life, the dynamic of its artworks, and the perception of its acts within the cultural context of Morocco. Yes.

It is with the same sense of an ethical and artistic ecology, learnt from this space, that I look back at this experience in order to share it with you. Welcome![6] It is this mode of ecological production that gives us the time. Each instant is acquired by listening and what follows is invested with the response.

[...]

Artworks act longer and beyond the time and the space of the exhibition.

The time of artworks is always beyond that of exhibitions and their space of activity is often larger, if it is not elsewhere.

Projects are constructed with this notion of freedom from the beginning, with the intention to act. I dreamed, I still dream, of testing this theory of freedom. The world should no longer erode individual freedoms, beliefs, convictions, and multiple ways of thinking.

The first exhibition that I organised in my apartment in Rabat is *JF_JH (Individualités)*. It is a demonstrative exhibition. Yes, it insists on the necessity of sharing spaces and of connecting the social context to the exhibition space.'

5. *JF_JH stands for Jeune Femme_Jeune Homme*. The exhibition title translates as *Young Woman_Young Man (Individualities)* [translator's note].

6. This text revisits the introduction and epilogue of the L'appartement 22 book. The formatting here distinguishes the previous text from this section, which is augmented by notes. The book's texts were written between 2002 and 2008. They are published and archived on the L'appartement 22 website, www.appartement22.com, and they have not been modified in the book. Certain passages, however, are underlined or blacked out to adapt them to the paper version of this archive. The texts written while traveling with QWERTY keyboards are not accented.

During these six years, the activities of the physical site in Rabat were increasingly produced in conjunction with the expedition project Le Bout Du Monde, where artists were invited to intervene outside of the exhibition space in discussion with curators and communities. The organisation became more and more fluid and the logistical ecology found a cruising speed that exceeded financial constraints. The question of financing became secondary in curatorial discussions, because spaces for encounters no longer force artists and curators to move around in order to act. Questions of the public and audience were also surpassed by those of the increasing importance of collaboration and co-production, and the political question was no longer asked through programmes but through projects that moved beyond strategies of resistance and distance, and that were inscribed in action instead.

When the platform for sharing is invested by a project and when the idea of interaction becomes an active proposal, the space of action becomes a zone of tension. At least on the organisational level, the autonomous character of artistic proposals creates a political interest among those who determine the limits in society. Unlisted activities, not previously authorised by the authorities, must draw their own limits, or at least trace the trajectory of their action.

'Ten October 2008 is a Friday not like any other, travelling. The aural landscape of the Avenue Mohamed V is still dominated by the cries of a generation of the educated and unemployed. I no longer spend much time here! Pedro just finished *Anytime Now*, filmed on L'appartement 22's balcony and co-produced in Bergen, Prishtina and Rabat, but it is possible to access it from anywhere in the world. The space is much larger. Clearly, it continues...

I dream about an art that changes the world:
- Do you hear me?
- Yes, always!
- [...]'

By starting this dialogue with a call I insist on the necessity of collaboration as a method for action. The cooperative is already operational and has allowed the productions of artworks and the organisation of meetings and exhibitions at L'appartement 22, as well as in more conventional spaces like the Brussels and Marrakech Biennales. The artistic creation that concerns my collaborators and myself is connected to the state of the world, and, above all, to the situation of the social space in which we find ourselves.

During the time that L'appartement 22 has existed, Rabat has become the most 'African' city in Morocco, even more so than the medina in Fez, which is a destination of pilgrimage for many Senegalese and Malians. The growth of the population in Rabat reflects the fact that young people from Mali, Senegal, and Benin travel North to change their lives, and blend in with the mass of diplomats and students who are already integrated in society. We see them more often in the street below L'appartement 22, sometimes with their Morocco born babies.

'This book is not a memoir of L'appartement 22. It is conceived as an autonomous space like L'appartement 22, R22, and each of the spaces, physical or symbolic, that have contained artworks and dreams. It is still a question of expression and not of Space.

Art's post-contemporary period[7] has seen enormous amounts of speculation. Faced with the domination of economic issues and spectacles, questions of art are too often obscured and remain unsaid or exist as allegorical representations. Contemporary art museums are already sites of heritage that conserve the artworks and the facts of the history of contemporary art and the period that will follow it. The notion of the post-contemporary period was an attempt to integrate everything that sat outside of the western idea of art and its ideals (tied to the market and war economy that predominates on every continent).

The majority of what the West has succeeded in integrating is interpretations and translations whose production is based on formal speculation and not on a symbolic or ecological contribution to the World.

The post-contemporary period has known the greatest re cycling of art's ideas and gestures. The forces of art are not necessarily defined by the space and for the allegedly global art system. Since the destruction of internal values, ethics, and aesthetics, the

7. See the symposium on 'The Issues and Networks of Art in the Post-Contemporary Period', organised by L'appartement 22 from 25 until 27 October 2007 in Rabat and from 29 until 30 October 2007 in Marrakech.

issues are elsewhere! The end of the end of history has already been integrated by the world, but only as a speculative narrative, not yet as a possibility.

The so-called "Western" space for art does not integrate that of "the rest of the world," which is described as "exotic" or strange. The latter is conveyed to make up for the lacks and desires of the former. The crucial question is how to get beyond readings that are inevitably comparative, since we know that the written history of art is a partisan monument.

By mentioning the 'general facebookisation of our activities' at the beginning of this text, I wanted to address the transformation of individualities into digital human profiles. I do not intend to attack the many tools of communication that offer numerous possibilities for real encounters and dialogue, but those that demand the supreme sacrifice and create the possibility for oligarchies to stop action at any moment – or at least to neutralise it – because they are the owners of these profiles. There is no model for the United Spaces of Art. Rather, we experience unique adventures navigating open spaces and are nourished by a pirate spirit. The persisting question throughout is how to face and reconsider the ecology of the resources of the fleets of international programmes that force our actions to be hidden behind their logos. It is a primordial reflection, because research methodologies and modes of action cannot be exported, especially not in the wake of colonial routes.

'The model of nation-states, an inheritance of colonialism, nationalism, and post-colonial interests, has no future in this "new world". The borders of nation-states are bound to disappear. Humanity only has a future by way of ecological behaviour with which it creates an experimental situation for life and not a situation acquired by searching for profits and exploiting the rest of the universe.

[...]

It is in this spirit of searching that, here and now, we work on the notion of "work", for example by searching for a formulation of reading the world. Artistic expression will find or re-find its sense at the moment when it is independent from the permanent pressure of market profits.

Throughout this unveiling, I confess that L'appartement 22 must create projects at the same time as it creates the tools for sharing its experiments.

The more I travel, the more I want to know the world. In 2008, I don't really live here anymore. Here, as elsewhere. The archive mixes with the real and the worlds send one another the same image of waiting. There is nothing to save. Everything must be built.

I still dream of an art that changes the world.
Wake up!'

On 10 October 2010, the Avenue Mohamed V is as noisy as ever, even more disorganised and confusing than usual. Yet another generation of educated and unemployed people joins the handicapped without rights and former combatants who were never compensated for their service. Groups of women mix with men and their demands resemble one another's. The cover of L'appartement 22's 2008 book, showing similar street scenes, is still a valid illustration of the mood and tension of society.

In the meantime, as an opposition to independent spaces, the large-scale and sick development and finances of real estate and tourism has reached Morocco. I see that auction houses and commercial galleries open every day in a frenzy of Art and Business that mixes luxury marketing, while copying and pasting of fragments of existing philosophical and exotic comments. Advertisements in this new, yet familiar, landscape completely ignore the noise and voices from the street.

The question of 'freedom?' needs constant addressing. The ongoing challenge is to create conditions for independent places to be sites that are open to the possibilities of reflecting on progress in a 'regressing' society. I do not agree with an institutional structure that is formatted by already existing social rules. The act of developing research methodologies and constructing tools for production and action is decided by the necessity for organisational 'independence'. The autonomy of the space should be detached from social conventions and communities of shared beliefs, which, like the belief in the nation, both come across as tribal. We need to write the histories of independent art spaces, because the spaces for exchange and sharing seem to be shrinking. Luckily virtual circuits open borders that are being closed in the real world. Together we are looking at how we can organise society in a different way than it is today. To me the reason for doing this is simple, and can be captured in one sentence. I would say: our country, like the world, has as many women as men, and yet the 2012 Moroccan government has only one female minister and this must change. So, rupture is essential, absolutely, but it is not the secret of creation, nor that of creativity.

To historicise it is essential to have a distance to heritage, and it is also within this awareness of historicising that we are able to prepare for outside threats and for what the future holds, in the tension of comings and goings, between knowledge and the perspective of action. As extras in this world, we are faced with the dilemma of presence versus active co-presence.

Rupture is also necessary because of how funding bodies and 'postcolonial' co-operations define spaces for creation and art centres. Such programmes ask you to initiate projects and exhibitions with artists from specific countries, preferably European - because they do not want to use the word nation - with an African artist, and sometimes they specify a sub-Saharan African - so as not to have to use the name of a formally colonised people. We have always refused. Of course, we have produced many projects with artists from all other continents, but never initiated by these national funding programmes. It is only after the artist is selected that it becomes possible to ask for assistance from these structures, but most of the time we have ended up supporting our projects through our own precarious economy.

It seems that art's history, including that of L'appartement 22 and other independent spaces, is simultaneously interacting with the history of social movements and with political directions that govern cultural programmes and with those that react to expressions and networks that are increasingly slippery and uncontrollable. A space is essentially defined by its vitality, even when we talk about geography or geology. A desert is not just a desert. It can be even more active than a volcano. Maybe it is similar to the pre-Islamic Arabian Peninsula's suspended poems, *Al Mu'allaqat*,[8] which defined temporary independent spaces, in village squares or on the surfaces of walls, ignoring the rules of the 'exhibition' that just imply ideas and activities for market profit.

8. Al Mu'allaqāt is the title of a group of seven long poems or qasida, written by some of the most well known poets from the sixth century. The title means *The Suspended Odes* or *The Hanging Poems*, the traditional explanation for which is that these poems were hung on or in the Ka'ba at Mecca.

Rupture is essential to any process of creation, both as a creative project and as an expression. In Classical Arabic poetry each verse is broken into two parts, thus including rupture as a key element of its construction. The creational potential lies in this necessary rupture. I would say rupture is a principle of comings and goings between knowledge and experience, consciousness and adventure. These are territories that are not entirely opposed, but that create the possibility for a certain kind of tension. This principle provokes questions of place and of time, our time and that of the memory of places. The succession of these verses repeats the poem's idea with new meanings and an image is built in the imagination, inspired by the external world or by bodily sensations.

In poetry, rupture is synonymous with respiration. In projects in society, it is synonymous with change. I continue to believe that art participates in the project of society and that it contributes to changing the world!

ACTIVE RECOLLECTION: ARCHIVING 'GROUP MATERIAL'

Julie Ault

'Each person who sits down to write faces not a blank page but his own vastly overfilled mind. The problem is to clear out most of what is in it, to fill huge plastic bags with the confused jumble of things that have accreted there over the days, months, years of being alive and taking things in through the eyes and ears and heart. The goal is to make a space where a few ideas and images and feelings may be so arranged that a reader will want to linger awhile among them [...] But this task of housecleaning (of narrating) is not merely arduous; it is dangerous. There is the danger of throwing the wrong things out and keeping the wrong things in [...]'[1]

Janet Malcolm

When the New York-based artists collaborative Group Material disbanded in 1996, I continued its representation through live narration and writings and responded to enquiries on a case-by-case basis. As the only founding member who remained until its conclusion I felt a responsibility to keep recounting the group's practice. Long-term member Doug Ashford did likewise. Group Material's cultural practice was temporal and the forms employed were ephemeral. When the group ceased its activities I was intent on preserving its ephemerality and *not* becoming history. Fearing a revisionist encapsulation in which conflicts and contradictions of collaboration are resolved in their representation, I resisted our work being defined or objectified in a monograph by an art historian, and reserved the right to cohere our history at some future point.

Following a decade of active narration I realised it was time to relinquish responsibility and control, and address Group Material's history with lasting effect. I needed to confront the material traces that had infiltrated every closet, cabinet and spare spot in my apartment, as well as the psychic traces that permeated memory. Collecting material saved by other group members as well, particularly the substantial amount of material saved by Doug Ashford, and joining it all together in an archive would permit access to Group Material in a more coherent way than had been possible before, and open the door for further historical representation.

Tackling the mission of recuperating Group Material involved gathering and organising the pool of material to constitute the archive,

1. Janet Malcolm, *The Silent Woman. Sylvia Plath and Ted Hughes*, Vintage, 1995, p. 205.

and simultaneously distilling from that body of information to make a book. While formalising the archive I sought to make Group Material public anew; the process was also conceived as a laboratory in which to investigate the logic, structure, implications and practice of an archive. I spent several months processing the material in its soon-to-be permanent home at the Downtown Collection at New York University: handling, reading and looking at every paper, image and item; taking notes, cross-referencing, recollecting and reflecting.(2) The more I reviewed the more deeply I understood the malleable and fallible nature of memory, and memory repeatedly threw documentary fact into question. Alternatively edified and mystified, the experience demonstrated the utter insecurity of the categories subjective and objective.

Looking back, I realise while telling the story of Group Material these past years I had unwittingly told some lies. This discovery occurred when encountering information in files that I had long since blotted from memory. Surprised, I read on and the divide between recollection and fact expanded. Certain retrieved information was basic while some signalled that Group Material was much more complex and debatable than I had meanwhile fabricated. It seems I had convinced myself that the streamlined storyline, which I repetitiously recounted for years, was accurate. My live narrations had fossilised into memorised short, medium, and long versions of the story. I repeatedly activated 'habit memory' and in the process, obstructed active recollection, which makes it possible to 'remount the slope of our past', and forge new relationships and meanings.(3)

Philosopher Paul Ricoeur reminds us that active recollection, or what he calls 'recollection memory', involves recognition, which memory out of habit does not.(4) Habitual memory exists in a mental filing cabinet, accessible on demand with the right call number.(5) Rupturing that dead-end circuit required purposely entering memory of a different

2. The Group Material Archive in the Downtown Collection can be viewed by appointment: Fales Library & Special Collections, Elmer Holmes Bobst Library, 70 Washington Square South, New York, NY 10012, USA. Phone: (212) 998-2596 Email: fales.library@nyu.edu.

3. Paul Ricoeur, *Memory, History, Forgetting*, translated by Kathleen Blamey and David Pellauer, The University of Chicago Press, 2004, p. 431. Ricoeur recounts two forms of memory Henri Bergson theorised in *Matter and Memory*, 'habit memory, which is simply acted out and lacks explicit recognition, and recollection memory, which is not without declared recognition.' [Ricoeur].

4. Ibid, p. 336.

5. 'Memory no longer consists in recalling the past but in actualising what has been learned and stored in a mental space. In Bergsonian terms, we have crossed over to the side of habit memory', ibid., p. 62.

order, 'present memory', as part of the larger process of apprehending, relearning and gaining fresh insight into Group Material through archiving and publishing.[6]

Of course documents and artefacts are not intrinsically truth-telling either; they are fragmentary and disconnected from context. Archives set the stage for history writing, yet they can mislead and even lie through omission. Essential pieces of information, which might answer questions and redirect research, are not necessarily tangible or archived.

Each aspect of cohering the archive and making the book *Show and Tell: A Chronicle of Group Material* (Four Corners Books, 2010 embodied specific and abstract purpose. A set of vexing questions fuelled the work. How does bringing documentation together imply shaping history and writing history? How do artefacts - whether material or informational - communicate? Can contexts be, in effect, communicated? What archival structure and practices will animate and complicate without over determining meanings? What tense is the archive? Where does the archive end? What can the collective subjective do when given the chance to write its own history? What is gained and lost in the process of subjecting ephemeral activities to conservation, and inducting them into history? What kind of suitable forms can be shaped to embody the historicising processes, gathered knowledge and diverse purpose that drive this inquiry? How to make what is missing evident as a layer of historicising? How does the subjective transform the material to a public sphere without manipulating it? Can one effectively challenge history writing while writing history?

Answering the question: 'Why did things happen like that and not otherwise?' requires turning past events into a 'followable story', which historian Hayden White distinguishes from historicising a *completed* story. Chronicles are capable of telling followable stories, whereas timelines endeavour to answer other questions, which call for judgement: 'What does it all add up to?' 'What is the point of it all?'[7]

Chronicles and timelines both function as narrative armatures. Both modes are linear at heart but the informational reach of the timeline

6. I have borrowed the term 'present memory' from the title of a 2010 work by artist Alejandro Cesarco to suggest, in this instance, memory that is present that takes place in the present and makes present or represents the past, simultaneously, which can happen with live narration.

7. Hayden White, *Metahistory: The Historical Imagination in Nineteenth-Century Europe*, The Johns Hopkins University Press, 1973, p. 7.

format is potentially more global as it encompasses multiple lines of inquiry and is capable of bringing seemingly incompatible information into confrontation. Timelines make larger explanation and historical analysis possible. Chronicles impart events and sequence. Chronicles record rather than historicise.

Because Group Material had used the timeline format as an exhibition structure on occasion, the idea of organising the book as a timeline of Group Material's history was briefly contemplated, but was rejected for that same reason – it seemed potentially trite when set alongside the group's timeline exhibitions.[8] Group Material conceived of a timeline exhibition as a mapping scheme capable of generating immersive diagrams of past events and potential readings of cause and effect within which viewers could navigate constellations of information and in the process formulate history. Yet graphic and printed timelines tend to reduce and level information on a unified seamless platform indicating that narratives have already been established into consumable compressed history lessons.

As the above questions that stimulated reopening the case of Group Material indicate, the inclination was to avoid pronouncements such as: 'This is what Group Material was all about.' To this end a chronicle structure seemed ideal.

Show and Tell's main section comprised reprinted documents and images, with a guiding text running throughout. The chronicle takes its ingredients and methods from the archive, which embodies both private and public material. The making of the group as a specific context along with its structure and process is inseparable from its public creations, yet the bulk of existing representation focuses on the latter. *Show and Tell* widens the focus to include conveyance of internal workings in each layer of material that forms the book, and stresses aspects of the collaboration that would otherwise have been invisible.

Group Material comes to life through the archive. Working with the material, I was struck by the vividness and changing character of internal correspondence, minutes of meetings, exhibition proposals and press releases produced by the group. Emotional intensity is palpable

8. Group Material employed the timeline format as a research and structuring device for two exhibition projects. The first was 'Timeline: A Chronicle of US Intervention in Central and Latin America', 1984, PS1, New York, and the second was *AIDS Timeline* 1989, Matrix Gallery, University Art Museum, University of California at Berkeley, which had subsequent versions.

in early communiqués: proposals and press releases are bombastic, topics and debates of the times are glimpsed through language, and graphic design bespeaks period styles. A selection of documents is reprinted in their original form and scale in *Show and Tell.* They are valued as 'original language', which vividly conveys what we perceived we were doing at the time far better than something written from the distance of time would, whether by someone inside or outside the group. This material would commonly be considered source material for writing rather than substance for presentation. By design, the book encourages that the documents be regarded as primary texts rather than ancillary illustrations. This method situates readers *in the archive*, inviting a multiplicity of interpretation.

Contradictory evidence is at the heart of the archive and prominently figures in this portrayal of Group Material. A four-page incendiary letter titled, 'A PROPOSAL FOR LEARNING TO GET THINGS OFF OUR CHESTS; BEHAVIORS, DISCIPLINE AND OUR PROJECT', written by co-founder Tim Rollins to the group in 1980, is fully reprinted alongside documents that represent a more harmonious collaboration. Tim's letter rants and rails rhetorically. It evidences major clashes in the group's first months but it also shows how seriously he regarded the collaboration and articulates what was at stake for the group.

The guiding text that filters throughout the chronicle was conceived as a non-specific voice imparting otherwise inaccessible circumstances, facts and anecdotes alongside the archive materials. It represents a close reading and distillation of multiple documentation and composite memory. This text captions, reports, digresses and discloses, coalescing subjective and objective knowledge into a seamless voice that augments the material. A depersonalised present-tense mode is used, intended to situate readers in the times of events and suggest collective subjectivity, distinct from first-person retrospection. Trains of information such as the continuities and discontinuities of the group's composition, conflicts and contradictions endemic to its process, and how Group Material structured itself and financed its work run throughout.

While reading through Group Material's files I noted many interesting segments in all types of documents, initially regarding this as source material for the guiding text. The number of full documents that could be reproduced was limited by the book's budget, which led to creating a layer of diverse extracts varying in author, purpose, length and style.

Unified by typographic design treatment, these also filter throughout the chronicle.

Image wise, snapshots portraying the various members and incarnations of the group, although in some cases there are no photographs, and formal installation photography of the collaborative's forty-five projects are presented on equal footing.

The chronicle's carefully designed formal system stresses all the material as primary. The book's visual tone builds on Group Material's aesthetic style. Analogous to the decentralised thematic exhibition format the group advanced, the chronicle is thought of as an exhibition space in the form of a book.

In his work to categorise history writing White has pointed out that a key problem of the (objective) chronicle or chronology is the notion that events tell themselves, in lieu of a (subjective) narrator.[9] At first glance, the chronicle of Group Material does exactly that, given that artefacts, facts and anecdotes are made present through themselves and by grammatically articulating the past as present. The archive shows itself, albeit through the prejudiced curatorial eyes of its participant interlocutor(s). Narration is not absent in *Show and Tell* and the narrator is conceived and configured as a 'collective subjective', constituted by the group that once was, and a more abstract version of the amalgam Group Material, which is conjured to do the telling in the present.

The chronicle spotlights atmosphere; its close-range eye-level orientation conveys that the collaboration was serious and it was fun; a sociable context.[10] A photographic analogy is helpful: the book's perspective is akin to a ground-level human-scale way of looking, while perspective situated in larger historical discourse is comparable to an aerial, bird's-eye view. Each method omits: the ground shot includes only glimpses of surroundings, the longer view makes it difficult to see what's happening close-up - such as a social process.

Ricoeur distinguishes the effects of scale in history writing: 'What can be seen on a large scale are the developing forces. But what can be

9. Hayden White, 'The Value of Narrativity in the Representation of Reality', in W. J. T. Mitchell, ed. *On Narrative*, The University of Chicago Press, 1981, especially pp. 2–4.

10. The detailed data of the exhibition history near the book's end, of venues, institutions, places, participants and collaborators are coordinates that portray context and inscribe a larger field of action and social relations. The exhibition titles of documented work chart a compendium of concerns and objectives.

seen on a small scale - and this is the lesson of microhistory - are the situations of uncertainty within which individuals [...] attempt to orient themselves [...] Therefore, when you write macrohistory, you are more likely to work with determinisms, whereas when you work on microhistories, you have to engage indecisions, that is to say, indeterminism.'(11)

Emphasising actions and dynamics at ground level seeks to highlight social process over effect and judgement. This emphasis works to create a multivalent space that can be engaged and projected into and out from, a space to harbour multiple points of entry and identification, and rouse interest, inspire imagination, critical consciousness and analysis. Contemporaries who revisit the period through the lens of Group Material attend with their individual awareness and interests as well as with an expanse of cultural memory. Those who are less or un-familiar with Group Material's activity and context are invited in at eye level to witness actions and circumstances through recollection of evidence and memory, conveyed in a present-tense telling, which regenerates a fundamental sense of cultural agency.

Books tend to streamline material and position readers by imposing a point of view, that of the narrator. Framing or summarising from a post-mode of narration can potentially short-circuit viewers' processes of discovery and conclude rather than extend Group Material in the process. *Show and Tell's* chronicle is decentralised: it does not privilege one point of view - much like a decentralised Group Material exhibition environment in which there is no ideal view; all views are potentially ideal and multiple perspectives are spurred.

Revisionist and interpretive tendencies have been restrained in *Show and Tell* in favour of creating a useful documentary foundation and introduction to Group Material's archive. The organisation of the archive and the response to that process through the book provide a platform and base interpretation to use, negotiate and take issue with.

The modality used for the 'present representation of absent, past things'(12) is dictated by purpose. Faithfully representing the group (to ourselves) for the sake of articulation, conservation, mourning and regeneration, influenced the mode of *Show and Tell*. Cohering the archive in public, literally taking it out of our hands and making the book, are in part,

11. 'Memory, History, Forgiveness: A Dialogue Between Paul Ricoeur and Sorin Antohi', 10 March 2003.
12. Ricoeur, op. cit., p. 138.

formalities for mourning the death of the group and regenerating the ideals that underwrote its course.

On the local level, faithful resemblance is tested through recognition, by ringing true. Do we recognise Group Material in this book? Does the depiction do justice to personal and collective memory? Do those who participated in and encountered Group Material's projects in real time recognise and recollect? Turning past events into 'history' is only partly for those who remember. The prime social reason for reopening the case was to stimulate action in the present and future. Further affinity is aspired for. The seemingly opposing goals of being, on the one hand, recounted, and on the other hand, open-ended, beckoned. Because *Show and Tell* inaugurates Group Material's 'history', it has the ability to define what Group Material 'was all about'. Intentionality is implied in the details of the documentation presented, but it is not summarised retrospectively. The paramount intention to represent faithfully and generate affinity dictated the book's methods. In its collaborative essence, and through its exhibition practice, Group Material embodied decentralisation as it created contexts in response to precise conditions, conflicts and alliances. The objectives that guided Group Material to resist making declaratives in its practice in favour of fashioning multivocal forums guided the approach in the book. Avoiding historical contextualisation invites a multitude of individual and social interpretations by the book's users, along their own lines of understanding, instead of prescribed ones, in essence, making it possible for readers to do the work of interpretation and historicising themselves.

In the aftermath of cultural presence, any iteration of Group Material is by definition history. Interpretation is suffused in every moment of searching, curating, editing, assigning relevance and connecting dots between documents that constitute research, including not least, presenting. However, *Show and Tell* stops short of overt interpretation as an explicit means. Group Material could be historicised more broadly in relation to intellectual and cultural turns and social trends, including postmodernism, multiculturalism, feminism, etc.; but such framing risks sacrificing its particular dynamics. Grounding Group Material's portrayal within larger social frameworks, which, at the time, appeared to be limitless but have since been bounded and periodised by historicisation, is at odds with composing a historical representation to launch clearings so that social memory and imagination in its diversity might be generated.

In *Show and Tell* Group Material's status is meant to be protected as *untheorised historically.*(13)

Historical staging is blunt. Group Material would be one thing in relation to punk and another in relation to postmodernism or conceptual art, the 1980s, or activism. Framing devices can be changed like backdrops in a photo studio, to change the figure's appearance in relation to different settings. Given that the group did not delimit its practice or definitively identify with any particular movement, -ism, or classification, it would be somewhat arbitrary to fasten on to one historical scaffolding.

When local history is situated in or against a historicised context which is larger and pre-established as a subject/discourse, it is in danger of being absorbed. The larger configuration tends to 'explain' the micro-history of a specific group of people and their experiences, decisions and actions. The microhistory gets thematicised and rendered an illustration of larger phenomenon. Because of the tendency of historical context-ualisation to function as explanation, the position taken rejected *all* frameworks, to instead focus on one microhistory and its capacity to accentuate and register cultural conditions and change, through the lens of itself.

Consider, for instance, were Group Material to be historicised by multiculturalism. As soon as the term is put forward its potential to take over is expressed. It is true that Group Material was in itself hetero-geneous and reflected various multiplicities in its exhibitions. But this was not because of 'multiculturalism', it was because culture *is* multicul-tural. That society is made up of multiple cultures is an undeniable fact.(14) Culture was multicultural before the term multiculturalism was active in any arena.

Clearly I do not mean to diminish or denigrate any theoretical inquiry and articulation, or any lived experiences associated with multi-culturalism, postmodernism, or feminism, etc., including my own. The impetus is to question the consequences of sweeping up the works and investigations of any artist, writer or practitioner, into periodising models, intellectual debates or social movements at the expense of their potential open-endedness.

13. This was the stance I took as the book's editor, and was not a group decision.
14. I am speaking generally about the US.

There is paradox in situating a practice that sought to 'question the entire culture we have taken for granted'[(15)] and the master narratives and dominant institutions of that culture, within an anti-grand narrative, such as postmodernism - a 'discourse of delegitimation'.[(16)] In spite of its critical design, such discourse can function as an alternative account - a history of dissent, counterculture and of constellations of critical intellectual debate, that takes shape as a quasi-grand narrative of Opposition.[(17)] I do not mean to suggest that historians and theoreticians plan this course. Although Group Material sometimes portrayed culture as a battleground, for the most part, it sought to cut across such a territorialised notion of the cultural economy and of society, and to speak in terms of 'for' rather than 'against'. In the long term, Group Material did not speak the vocabulary of opposition or dissent so much as participation, agency and multiplicity. For Group Material to be recognised it needs to reinforce itself. *Show and Tell* refuses to speak in terms of oppositions. The apparent dichotomies of dominant and marginal, culture and counterculture, Left/Right, righteous and corrupt, aesthetic and political, etc., lost their soundness over time in practice. On behalf of Group Material, *Show and Tell* takes a less contrast-driven stance. By refusing to affirm such disunion in representation *Show and Tell* stays true to the group's history of lived experience and does not further replicate polarising notions of culture.

15. 'Our project is clear. We invite everyone to question the entire culture we have taken for granted.' Group Material inaugural statement, 1980. Reprinted in Julie Ault, ed., *Show and Tell*, Four Corners Books, 2010, p. 23.

16. Referring to Lyotard's argument in *The Postmodern Condition* that the discourses of legitimation have failed, and then talking about the 'grand narratives' proposed by Christian Theology and Marxism which have lost their credibility: 'We are engaged, whether we like it or not, in a discourse of delegitimation.' Ricoeur, op. cit., p. 313.

17. 'As microhistory has already verified, the initial benefit of a variation in scale is that it shifts the accent to individual, familial or group strategies that call into question the presupposition of submission by social actors on the bottom rank to social pressures.' Ricoeur, op. cit., p. 218.

113 – 121

DEFINING THE ENEMY AND POST-FORDIST BUSINESS AS USUAL

What, How & for Whom/WHW

Terry Gilliam's *Brazil*, a dystopian black comedy from 1985, depicts a future society more or less organised around terrorism, or, more precisely, against terrorism, and in an astonishingly far-sighted way in many of its details it predicts things that really did happen twenty-something years later. In a TV interview that takes place at the beginning of the film, the Minister of Finance is asked how it is possible that the terrorists have been active for 13 years already, and his answer is 'beginners' luck'. This potentially also applies to many collectives, and could be the best explanation for how they are able to persist with their work for decades, often against a backdrop of rather unfavourable social circumstances and with increasing precariousness.

This could also be how things stand with WHW. Our 'beginners' luck' started at the end of the turbulent 1990s, and the collective's practice developed against the background of specific moments of urgency as they played out in the so-called 'post-transitional', 'normalised' social and cultural context of Croatia in the aftermath of the conflict that followed the break-up of Yugoslavia, on the outside borders of the European Union. The shifts and transformations of this context have influenced the way in which the collective's position has been expressed through exhibitions and projects organised in the course of the last twelve years.

Since 1999 the work of WHW has been set against specific intensities characterised by cul-de-sacs, dislocations, contradictory movements and a series of changes that completed the transition from Fordism to post-Fordism. Thanks to its flexibility and manageability, an openness to various forms of cooperation and networking, and, most importantly, the rise of a knowledge-based economy built on social and cultural capital, art was in the course of this period assigned a central place in the economy of the new post-Fordist regime. At the same time, the instrumentalisation of public funding and the non-profit sector as dominant material basis for contemporary art production increasingly took over, and dissipated critical discourses and art practices within the rhetoric of daily politics. The attempts to navigate pressures brought about by these transformations and their particularities in Croatian, post-Yugoslav, and wider international contexts, and to create strategies to deal with issues of betrayal, cooptation and assimilation have certainly been crucial in the continuation of WHW's practice in the last few years.

If we talk about the beginnings of what we today call Post-Fordism as it pertains to the practice of WHW, when 'Even so unproductive activities as acting, speaking and thinking are forced to undergo commodification or reproductive socialisation, or they are socially marginalized',[1] we could situate it at the very beginnings of the processes that in the 1990s went under the name of 'transition', in what Nebojša Jovanović, a psychoanalyst from Sarajevo, described as transitology, whose main problem 'lies precisely in the Western doxa of democracy as the only solution for post-communist problems.'[2] This process could also be seen as a culmination of a long and gradual process of abandonment of socialist self-management in Yugoslavia,[3] which, as philosopher Gal Kirn argues, itself contained seeds of many elements of what we today call post-Fordism, starting with the first market reforms of self-management in 1965, and an important emphasis on knowledge realised through a series of educational reforms introduced from the 1970s onwards, that Kirn regards as a Bologna declaration *avant la lettre*, a form of managerial-bureaucratic synthesis that engaged to improve efficiency of the economy and the labour market.[4] These elements are also crucial to understand the subsequent wars in Yugoslavia, which were not a consequence of some ancient religious and national hatred, as they were often presented through the comfortable Western clichés, but a result of social transformation that abandoned the socialist project and violently dismantled socialism in a kind of shock doctrine, or what Naomi Klein calls 'a strategy of neo-liberalism gaining momentum through exploiting crisis it creates', starting with Chile after the Pinochet coup in 1973, continuing through the former Soviet Union and countries of the Eastern Bloc, the Asian crisis in the late 1990s, and many other places and wars, including Yugoslavia in the 1990s.

1. Gorazd Govačić, 'Arendt's Critique of Marx, and Post-Fordist Socialism: What is the Sense of Economy?, in Gal Kirn, ed., *Post-Fordism and Its Discontents*, Jan van Eyck Academie/Workers'-Punks' University and Peace Institute/b_books, 2010, p. 113.
2. Nebojša Jovanović, 'A Prejudice in Culture', eipcp – European Institute for Progressive Cultural Policies, September 2000, available online at. http://eipcp.net/transversal/1100/jovanovic/en.
3. After breaking up with Stalinist politics and the USSR in 1948, the People's Assembly of Yugoslavia adopted the Law on Workers' Self-management in 1950. The law created workers' councils, that had authority within each working collective, but whose power was ultimately defined and controlled by the Party. Self-management in Yugoslavia was seen as the basis of the 'withering away of the state' and a phase of transition towards a communist society. On the one hand, it created a hybrid of various forms of economic organisation that enabled direct democracy at lower levels of production. On the other, the combination of a planned economy, a manifestation of Party control, and market economy, especially after the market reforms of 1965, brought about the deep chasm between proclaimed and realised ideals of socialism.
4. Gal Kirn, op. cit., pp. 253–305.

From today's perspective, the thematic threads, procedures and obsessions that run through all of WHW's projects can be seen as part of the politics that were built around what the philosopher and political scientist Susan Buck-Morss calls 'defining the enemy', in her book *Dreamworld and Catastrophe, the Passing of Mass Utopia in East and West*, in which she compares collective imaginaries of capitalism and socialism as virtual worlds that through the process of making them real become the social project. In her argument this opens up a possibility for a 'wild zone of power' in which the claim to the monopoly of violence can never be democratic, and which is intrinsic to every state, both Western democracies and former socialist states. This certainly applies to Yugoslavia, whose dissolution was followed by a series of wars that in Buck-Morss's argument follow logically from collective identity implying ethnic homogeneity, when she claims 'fascism is not aberrant to the nation-state imaginary, but rather its limit case. Within a political imaginary where ethnic-national distinctions between "we" and "they" set the terms of the possibility of war, the concept and hence the real possibility of genocide remain necessarily a part of the picture.'(5) This is - obviously - what had happened in Yugoslavia, with some of its consequences still being discussed at the European court for war crimes in The Hague.

Buck-Morss's position on defining the enemy as the act that brings collectives into being and that when applied to collective identities includes the monopoly to violence, in an inverted form pertains to WHW, because as individuals we found ourselves exposed to violence, and as a collective constituted ourselves *against* it. In a metaphoric sense WHW came into being through defining the enemy from a shared political position that argued against nationalism as the social glue that connected Croatian society during the 1990s. In our view, nationalism was the basic element around which the main social and political forces were formed after the disintegration of Yugoslavia, and that sat at the centre of the change of the social system, from socialist self-management to a neo-liberal society of parliamentary democracy and market economy. Simply put, our projects were aimed at exposing nationalistic ideologies that were permeating public discourses and were widely used in anti-communist rhetoric that justified an identity-based understanding of

5. Susan Buck-Morss, *Dreamworld and Catastrophe, the Passing of Mass Utopia in East and West*, MIT Press, 2002, p. 17.

culture in an exclusive way. We tried to counter the silently accepted notion of a Year Zero, which proclaimed that history started with the establishment of Croatian independence, with the fulfillment of '1000 years of national longing', which in its turn paved the way for an inappropriate tolerance and even glorified the whole spectrum of right-wing options – from just being 'proud nationalist' to openly supporting the fascist quisling Croatian state of post-World War II, or war crimes 'committed for the homeland' during the most recent war.

This basic question of how to oppose processes of violent formation of 'national culture' has always been at the core of our activities, while we have simultaneously tried to address the changes of context, for example in a series of projects that were specifically dealing with the notion of normalisation, through which we also attempted to address our own complicity in these processes. We understood normalisation as a process following the end of openly nationalistic governments across the countries of former Yugoslavia, which won elections on the promise of advancing towards the 'normalcy' of Western late-capitalist societies, as welfare states in which human rights would be fully respected. We saw this normalcy as a product of the Western neo-liberal ideology, where questions about the price of that 'normalisation' were never asked, and consequently, all its ugly results – unemployment, poverty, crime, the widening of class differences, the decrease of social and health security, a conservative backlash, the rise of ethnic, racial and sexual intolerance etcetera – have so far not been understood as regular products and symptoms of the liberal-capitalist system, but as mere 'side-effects'. 'Side-effects' was the title of the exhibition we curated in the Salon of the Museum of Contemporary Art in Belgrade in 2003, which was the first post-war exhibition in Belgrade that included contemporary artists from Croatia – although not only from Croatia – which was of course the very sign of normalisation itself.

We worked around the questions of normalisation for several years through a series of diverse projects, dealing with notions of collective amnesia, anti-fascist heritage, relationships to monuments, questions of abstraction and modernisms, through for instance the exhibition 'Normalization, dedicated to Nikola Tesla' in 2006. Nikola Tesla (1856–1943), a Serbian scientist from Croatia who died as an American citizen, fell from national hero to persona non grata during the 1990s in Croatia. In 2006, the 150th anniversary of his birth was celebrated in grand style, and he became a powerful rhetorical symbol of the political reconciliation between Croats and Serbs. We argued that the celebratory inclusion of Tesla in the narrative of national culture presupposes the exclusion of public reflections on the war period and unsolved traumatic processes of the 1990s, including the fact that in 1995 between 150,000–250,000 Serbs were expelled during the military action called 'Storm', which abruptly 'solved' the Croatian conflict through the territorial re-distribution of ethnicities and which marked the end of the war.(6)

Obviously, since the beginning of our collaborative work the political and social context have changed, just as our working conditions and circumstances: from an informal self-organised group based on friendship to a complex partnerships, permanent gallery space, increased international visibility and an ever-increasing amount of bureaucracy. But the main motivation of the collective, its aim to work against the 'wild zone of power', has remained constant. We have always attempted to connect our projects to broader questions of a so-called European identity and international solidarity, based on an exploration of a discourse of East versus West, with which we have maintained very complicated relations. This need for building international platforms was expressed in almost all of our projects and has been running through numerous collaborations with artists and cultural workers from countries of former Eastern Europe, as well as from other 'ghost geographies' that are to various degrees struggling with their imposed and/or internalised 'marginal' position in relation to the Western or Soviet project of modernism – such as the Middle East, Central Asia, the Caucasus – in which contemporary art relates with a certain tension to ideas of the 'authentic' and 'indigenous' national cultures. We have focused on tentative encounters with the lived experiences of multiple, experimental modernisms, and on critical investigations of hegemonic relations of cultural geo-politics, possible oppositional strategies, as well as questions of discrepancy between local and international receptions. Throughout the diverse projects concerned with these issues, our background in a local Croatian context and our anti-nationalistic position has strongly determined our work, and this is what could be described as the 'idea' of our collective, in the sense of the term as used in the essay 'Group As Bearer of Ideas' by Siegfried Kracauer, who preceded what later would be called cultural studies and

6. The number of refugees that left Croatia in August 1995 is highly contested to this day – Croatian sources acknowledge the number of 90,000 refugees, while the UN estimates it at 150,000, and Serbian sources at 250,000.

whose essays, which were published in Germany during the Weimar republic in the *Allgemeine Zeitung*, today certainly make for timely reading. In this particular text Kracauer writes about how corporeality of a socially effective idea is produced by individualities that make up a group, carefully delineating 'the communities of life and fate from those groups that actually bear ideas', and showing how the idea imposes itself on a group and in its turn creates individualities.(7)

The dynamics of a group was at the core of our project 'Collective Creativity', which we realised in the Kunsthalle Fridericianum in Kassel in 2005, but at that time we were more interested in how a 'Collective is much more than a sum of its parts', as Jon Hendricks, member of Guerilla Art Action Group has described it; how the instrumentality of collective work is always smaller than the surplus of enjoyment in collective work. The main focus of the exhibition 'Collective Creativity' was on different forms of collective artistic work evolving around certain social tensions that serve as a common axis around which various group activities are being organised. We focused on a duration of a group as something that gives it a substance, in distinction and opposition to temporary collaborations, which at the time were all the hype as part of the so-called 'relational aesthetics', and which were much discussed in the art world, often even as intrinsically politically effective and challenging the implication of art in maintaining the status quo. This enthusiasm, which from today's perspective looks very much like a sign of the times, has lost much of its appeal with the rapid advance of neo-liberal transformation in recent years. In this light Kracauer's rather pessimistic writing on the life-span of a group, its involvement with ideas and their duration assumes a new importance. He writes: 'let us assume that at the time of the group's founding the members set up a hard and fast program containing all the demands to be made of the current state of reality according to the idea that generated the group. While the group individuality then goes about intervening in reality according to the terms of this program, that reality itself changes (to some extent also as a result of the group's actions) and new situations arise that demand a different stance on the part of the group.'(8) But he continues to write about a group's gradual withdrawal from the idea as a result of immersion in reality, continuation by inertia, yearning for the assertion of power: 'The idea

7. Siegfried Kracauer, *The Mass Ornament*, Harvard University Press, 1995, pp. 144.
8. Siegfried Kracauer, opt cit., p. 160.

takes sublime revenge on the now powerful group that has slipped from its grasp.'[9] For a collective, there is a constant need to rethink the singularity of each particular situation in relation to its adopted, and after a while standardised methods, and to try to embrace caution and deliberation as an antidote to the oppression of one's own well-rehearsed efficiency in the face of precarious times.

To a large extent, six or seven years ago, when we were exploring the emanicipatory potentials of collective work, we could ignore the question of constant renegotiation of our values in relation to power, as well as the conditions of producing and presenting critical art practices within the globalised institutional framework of 'major international art institutions'. Our practice, after all, promptly returned from Kassel's Fridericianum to the precarious, and rather tiny space of the city-owned Gallery Nova in Zagreb. The same question became a topic after we curated the Istanbul Biennial in 2009, certainly our internationally most visible project, in which we summarised many of our constant concerns in the exhibition entitled 'What Keeps Mankind Alive'.[10] Through the exhibition, we emphasised that today, like had happened previously, one of the consequences of the economic crisis has been the massive shift to the right of the (European) electoral body, and that the outcome of the crisis depends on our activities or passivities. The exhibition did not claim to be 'Marxist', as it did not refer to the central concepts of Marxism of Party and proletariat, but it recalled the 'communist hypothesis', as Badiou would call it. The exhibition was met with considerable criticism from many sides and the most immediate commentators distanced themselves from its political thrust, either through open attacks, or in a more subtle ways through patronising and dismissive praise, but nevertheless, and somewhat contradictory, often praising the 'quality of the works' and admirable research behind it. In general, the exhibition enjoyed a reasonable level of success. Following Brecht, this success can be measured only in tension with its impact, or, as Heiner Müller put it: 'One is always overtaken by success before a real impact can occur. As long as a thing works it is not successful, and when success is there

9. Ibid, p. 167.
10. The exhibition took its title from *The Three-Penny Opera*, written in 1928 by Bertolt Brecht, in collaboration with Elisabeth Hauptmann and Kurt Weill. The concept of the exhibition relied on this play and its critical thematisation of the process of the redistribution of ownership within bourgeois society, Brecht's method in general, and the parallels between the liberal economy and its relation to social consensus in 1928 and the present times, as the economic crisis is exploding throughout the world.

then the impact is over.'[11] This lesson for us certainly intensified the questions on the duration and role of a group, which Kracauer posed, although the positions are of course not as clear-cut as they are in his analysis, and gaining the position of power is precluded by increasing precarity and pressures on cultural production, especially cultural production to the left of the political spectrum, which is certainly not characteristic for just Croatia.

While the question of how to navigate away from the dreadful course of events in Kracauer's times proved to be self-fulfilling prophecies that played themselves out in the historical nightmare of Nazism and World War II, at the present moment, when we are witnessing the rise of the right-wing policies - in the Netherlands, Hungary, Finland, Sweden, Austria, the European Parliament, to name just a few - it has become increasingly urgent. Kracauer's answer was to endorse the position of waiting. One could hardly be blamed for objecting that in the case of Kracauer's and his generation this waiting did not end up all too well, but perhaps there really is not much choice left in today's society focused on services and consumption, where the attempts towards reconstruction of the public sphere stay confined within market conditions, with critique being internalised and institutionalised, produced through a self-referential and self-perpetuating disciplinary field of the art system. In a more positive light, this is a moment of strategic waiting that should be seen as more stubborn and insistent rather than as passive, and that can be translated into a continuity, an enduring beyond the stretching point. It is a waiting that involves embracing openness to test modalities of art production and critical thinking within and at the edges of the existing systems, and sustaining it over a long period of time, because, as history teaches us, bad times could last very long.

11. Heiner Müller, in 'Intelligence without Experience, Interview with Haroun Farocki', first published in *Filmkritik*, No. 293, May 1981, republished in Heiner Müller, *Germania*, semiotext(e), 1990.

122 – 134

ALL THE WRONG EXAMPLES

Jan Verwoert

In the arts, the question of self-organisation usually presents itself in very concrete terms: either you do it, or you drown. We are free to self-organise. But if we don't, our lives tend to fall apart very quickly. It doesn't make too much of a difference these days whether you work as an independent artist, a freelance curator or critic or in a smaller arts institution. The need to create and maintain the economic conditions for the continuation of your practice is a daily challenge. So you organise yourself. Alone and together with others. Which can be fun and generate a sense of shared freedom, but it nonetheless always remains contingent on a sense of struggling for survival. What gives you a sense of freedom and empowerment one day, on the next will remind you that there is no other option. How are we to live with this contradiction? Let's broaden the question: What forces shaped the current situation? Why does talking about self-organisation feel so contemporary? And why do we treat it as a social perspective, when we know it is a material need?

If we look at the bigger picture, the political figures that have been most influential for how the concept of self-organised practice has been interpreted in contemporary European culture are Vladimir Putin, Silvio Berlusconi and Tony Blair.[1] While they were in office they, openly or covertly, used the power of the state to further dismantle society and to raise the pressure on everyone to organise the conditions of social survival themselves: much to the advantage of those who were in positions to benefit from the deregulation of the social order, and to the disadvantage of those who still have to rely on their rights as citizens for existential support. Each of these politicians, however, gave a different spin to the manner in which they represented, legitimised and enforced the transformations. Let's compare:

Putin

In the Central European context, 1989 marks a year of transition, not necessarily of change. In the years preceding this date, many societies inside the Soviet Union had effectively already ceased to function as societies. With the state apparatus in control, yet on the verge of collapse, with national economies on their knees and the social morale at an all-time low, people knew from everyday experience that there

1. I would like to thank Federica Bueti for provoking me to address the topic in this way, and for her perceptive comments on the rise and fall of Silvio Berlusconi.

was no support to be expected from state institutions. Citizenship gave you no benefits. Consequently, people started to self-organise, out of disenchantment with society, in order to make ends meet. In Polish the term for doing so is *robić swoje*: to work for yourself.(2) The final years of State Socialism in this sense became a re-education camp for teaching onself the survival techniques which, after the collapse of the regime, were to define the new status quo of turbo-capitalism.(3) So effectively all these techniques had already been rehearsed and incorporated when the new order was installed.

While it emerges from a cut of all ties with society at large, the art of working for yourself intensifies the relation to the social in a different way - as corruption effectively was the means through which you 'organised' what you needed - and in GDR parlance to 'organise' something literally meant to find ways of procuring the goods and tools for everyday purposes by unofficially talking to people and entering into deals with them. And as the social bonds tightened around you, the more you inevitably became entangled and indebted to your collaborators. At a recent conference,(4) artist Olaf Nicolai described this practical logic of self-organisation as embedded in a 'godfather economy' in which all attempts to get something done for yourself would increase your personal dependence on others. For example, how organising heating for your flat would make it mandatory to drink yourself stupid with the plumber first, so that he would feel sufficiently indebted to you to come and unofficially treat you to a heater, as a personal favour.

The power of Putin is based on the fact that he managed to both incoporate *and* dissimulate the very spirit of this godfather economy of self-organised life. On the one hand, he is the godfather incarnate: the man to whom you must talk to get things organised. He is the devil you know. On the other hand, however, he also embodies the 'new man', not as oligarch, but as a Russian, a vigorous patriot. As a former KGB man he belongs to a class of people which profited most from the transitional years: as they had priviledged access to information, infrastructure and

2. The notion of *robić swoje* was introduced to me by Anna Rubinowicz-Gründler, journalist for the Polish newspaper *Gazeta Wyborcza* at the time of our conversation in 2004.

3. Polish critic and curator Łukasz Ronduda described the years of transition to me in this manner in terms of going through an experience of physical re-education, in conversation in 2005.

4. 'Intangible Economies', conference hosted by Antonia Hirsch for *Fillip* magazine at GreyChurch Collection & Project Space, Vancouver, Canada, November 2011.

resources in their former position within the military or inside state-owned companies, people of Putin's class had an invaluable head start. They effectively already had their hands on what was supposedly public property, so when the system collapsed, they could take overnight what they had been controlling in the name of an already decrepit state.

To *mask* the fact that the new men are the old men, however, is what Putin succeeded in doing much better than others did. By punishing and expropriating individual oligarchs, almost wilfully, he publicly disavowed his membership of this new class and presented himself as a strong Russian statesman. He did what kings traditionally do to their aristocracy: spread fear among them through random sanctions against individual members. Having a figure like Putin as the head of the state confirms what everyone knows, that in this state there is 'no such thing as society' at large – and that the personalised godfather economy defines the way in which social ties are forged. The confirmation of reality as is, however, is instantly transfigured into an image of nationalist pride, as the man who holds the power – of his new class – to exploit all, presents himself as the man who embodies the strength of the whole people to rise above.

Berlusconi and Blair

Berlusconi and Blair performed a similar operation. As facilitators to the installation of a new order, they sought to make people love the principles of their own exploitation. And their voters seemed more than happy to comply. Ironic as it may seem, the tendency of giving the power over public affairs to those who are most likely to use it against you, has a long tradition. In German there is even a proverbial expression to describe it: *Den Bock zum Gärtner machen* [making the goat the gardener]. Much of Theodor W. Adorno's political philosophy could be understood as an attempt to analyse this need to identify with one's oppressors. (In place of the German expression, he uses a similar Italian phrase, *il servo padrone* [the servant master] to allude to this social mimicry.[5]) Roughly speaking, one could summarise Adorno's analysis like this:

5. Theodor W. Adorno, *Minima Moralia* (1951), Verso, 2005, p. 182. Adorno and Horkheimer's critique of the dialectics of englightenment is largely based on this notion: The need to validate existing structures of domination as an unquestionable given, they argue, expresses itself in the readiness to embrace any modern myth (or charismatic figure) that makes the status quo seem natural. See Max Horkheimer & Adorno, *Dialectic of Enlightenment* (1947), Stanford University Press, 2002.

A sense of comfort can be garnered from siding with those who exploit you. When you invest faith in an exploitative relationship, it will feel as if there was sense to it. That way you prevent yourself from facing the cruel fact that your current suffering may be *in vain*! The easiest way to make your plight seem justified therefore is to vote for those who appear to understand your troubles best - because they cause them. By supporting the system that exploits you, you can at least live with the feeling that all is in order, even if the order is working against you. Berlusconi mastered the art of replacing the gardener with the goat. People loved him for being the cunning self-serving trickster (who knows how to 'work for himself') which they themselves have to be to get by, and loved him even more for succeeding, better than they can, in making money and having power.

The fact that the money he made was the money he took from those who empowered him to do so by voting for him, seemed to have little bearing on people's affection for what he represented. After all, he only did what most people would have done if they had been in his position. Only he did it better than anyone else. The open cynicism expressed in making someone who rips off society the head of the state adds to the liberatory effect of siding with the winner: you don't even have to pretend that there was a social morale. What a relief! Berlusconi gave people permission to do what they were doing anyway. Only now they could do it without feeling bad about it: organise things *for* themselves and keep their wealth to themselves, rather than share wealth with society (for seriously, who would want to pay taxes to a society run by a joker?) As a result, the current financial crisis in Italy is a crisis of the state. People have money and property. Only the state is bankrupt. The only way to really change this situation would be to give people reasons to literally *re-invest in the concept of society at large* rather than in the feeling of there being no alternative to self-organising their survival.

Rhetorically, at least, Blair attempted to restore faith in the social. The manifesto *Europe: The Third Way*[6] which Blair co-authored with Gerhard Schröder, who was then Chanellor of Germany, is known to largely be based on the thoughts of Anthony Giddens. Its main premise, however, can in turn be traced back to the teachings of modern economist Joseph Alois Schumpeter (1883-1950) who portayed entrepreneurship

6. Tony Blair and Gerhard Schröder, *Europe: The Third Way*, released on the 8th June 1999.

as an inherently social practice. Schumpeter's reasoning runs something like this: Any self-made man depends on the help of others to achieve his goals. Setting up an enterprise therefore is a collaborative creative effort. Only when the entrepreneur has the social skill set to motivate a small community of professionals to work together, will he succeed. The marriage of neo-liberal and social democratic thought that Blair sealed in his manifesto was possible on the grounds that the social democrat boyscout ethos of 'Altogether now! Let's get organised!' is highly compatible with the grassroots spirit of starting one's own business together with others.

Arguably, there is an honorable tradition of families building up a business over generations and running it with a commitment to business ethics and social responsibility to their local community. The irony, however, lies in the fact that precisely this tradition (appraised by Schumpeter) was being aggressively dismantled in the days of Blair, despite the latter's vocal attempts to ressurect it. In the 1990s the popularity of the shareholder system increased to such an extreme extent that everyone felt entitled to gamble on stocks. The more external power shareholders have over a company, however, the less internal power the company owners have to make responsible decisions. Long-term planning becomes impossible when the need to keep your stockholders from deserting ship and selling their stocks forces you to do whatever it takes to present short-term successes. The very basis for socially responsible entrepreneurship was therefore being eroded by the very logic of what Blair was promoting: 'Every man an entrepreneur!' effectively meant 'Everybody gamble!' (I vividly remember a conversation with a London taxi driver advising me that it was a good time to invest in property in Poland now...) The no-holds-barred attitude to betting on the market, promoted as entrepreneurial, as we have now seen, destroys enterprises and family fortunes together with the conscientious decision-making capacity that would have qualified the traditional entrepreneur as a responsible member of society and good citizen.

Blair forcefully advanced the idea that people must work for themselves, yet he disguised it as a social-democratic ideal of grassroots social productivity. He reminded people that the state apparatus cannot do what only communities can and that it was fundamentally the people's own task to organise the social. A central passage in the *Third Way* manifesto reads:

'The belief that the state should address damaging market failures all too often led to a disproportionate expansion of the government's reach and the bureaucracy that went with it. The balance between the individual and the collective was distorted. Values that are important to citizens, such as personal achievement and success, entrepreneurial spirit, individual responsibility and community spirit, were too often subordinated to universal social safeguards.'

'Too often rights were elevated above responsibilities, but the responsibility of the individual to his or her family, neighbourhood and society cannot be offloaded on to the state.' (7)

The thought that the social should be reborn out of the spirit of every person getting their game on then culminates in the demand: 'We want a society that celebrates successful entrepreneurs just as it does artists and footballers, and which values creativity in all spheres of life.'(8) Society at large is here portrayed in terms of a media audience or cultural public that identifies itself through its heroes and interprets personal initiative as a social virtue.(9) But who are the people that form society? Are they all heroes? A people made up of entrepreneurs, footballers and artists? Wouldn't you want to be part of that society? As upbeat as this promise sounds, as obviously phantasmatic it is. There is no such thing as such a society. In fact, the more Blair charges the concept of the social with the dynamic language of people creatively organising their own community, the more vacuous the meaning of the term 'society' becomes. The macro level of political consciousness that defines society at large becomes impossible to address once the micropolitics of individual initiative and community spirit are presented as if they, by themselves, could provide the structures for how a modern society is to be organised as a whole. Passing off the micro as the macro is a rhethorical slight of hand which practically disguises that crucial

7. Tony Blair and Gerhard Schröder, *Europe: The Third Way*, released on the 8th June 1999.

8. Ibid, no page numbers.

9. Much of the critique of the *Third Way* Manifesto I summarise here, were thoughts collectively formed and discussed in a series of workshops at the Academy of Umeå in 2004 conducted together with Søren Grammel which resulted in the collaborative student project Academy of Umeå Project Group: *We Invite All*, presented in the exhibition *Whatever happened to Social Democracy* at the Rooseum, Malmö in 2005.

decisions are still being taken on the macro-level: namely the decision for the state to step back and leave the field to the market forces and those who command them.

Now What?

Blair eventually fell out of favour with the voters. Berlusconi was forced out of office. Putin is still in power but faces protests. Those who played their part in justifying the new order of capitalism by masking its workings seem to have lost their credibility, finally. Their ideological shadowplay seems to have reached the point where, through overuse, its tattered mechanics become far too obvious to ignore. In Italy, the current response is to default back to pragmatism and hand power over to a certified technocrat. For Germany and arguably for the European Union in general, Angela Merkel has come to embody a new style of ostentatiously 'post-ideological' politics, interpreting her role as that of a pragmatic manager and negotiator in a scenario of national crisis. No promises. No show. No lies. Merkel could be applauded for not presenting herself as the living justification of unjust conditons. At the same time, however, her unconditional pragmatism does indeed also communicate a strong ideological message in its own right. Namely, that politics can never do more than *react* to economic situations that other players create. Perhaps it is an illusion that politicians struggling with the status quo of socio-economic conditions could ever do more than respond to problems, and actually *shape* society. And maybe any political philosophy that promises to open up such perspectives for shaping societies is therefore delusional, almost by definition.

Be that as it may. But one thing should also be clear. An absence of perspectives equally entails a total lack of criteria for rejecting the current conditions and demanding a better society. After all, the rise of Berlusconi could conceivably be understood as an outcome of such a lack of perspectives and general political fatigue. After all, why would people make a petty-bourgeois anarchist the head of state if not for the simple reason that he embodied the disenchantment with politics *as a form of* politics and, with liberating obscenity, demonstrated that, if there is nothing to believe in, you might as well just believe in yourself. To counter this type of popular cynicism, one would need to raise the stakes. No dreams. No criteria. Low stakes. Assuming, however, that the stakes are higher than ever, how are we to formulate them?

How the Isms Work in Art

The irony is that in the art field the rhetorics and leadership styles of Blair, Berlusconi and Putin have had tangible effects, despite the fact that there are obviously no countries to be governed or voters to be coaxed into supporting national politics. Blairism was (or still remains) highly popular as a management philosophy in art institutions: a whole vocabulary of micropolitical engagement and grassroots communitarian ethics has been mobilised in recent years, not merely to explain what curating exhibitions and shaping institutions could be about, but very much also to motivate people to get - and stay - involved in art. Often enough, however, the appraisal of micropolitics on the level of participatory engagement obscures the fact that macropolitical decision-making power still exists, and that it lies in the hands of some people rather than others.

True, it takes communities to change institutions from within, and so ethos matters! But the uncanny inner logic of institutional power structures tends to persist on a macro-level, especially when, rather than being openly addressed, power asymmetries are glossed over through the invocation of communal morale: there is a limit to how far you can go in making your collaborators feel they are part of a self-organised grassroots organisation, when they might just be underpaid freelance contributors (without contracts or securities) to what, after all, remains an institution with a budget that at least gives those who run it a secure source of income. The point where the Blairist bubble bursts is usually when the institutional dynamics supersede the personal terms in which a working relationship may have been negotiated - because the person in charge stops caring or, timewise, cannot even manage to sustain the pretense of personal loyality - and you realise: No, this is neither the boyscouts nor a self-organised social movement. This is an art institution that depends on gratuitous outside contributions from artists and intellectuals in order for it to exist.

The Berlusconi principle helped to pave other careers in the arts. A formula that works just as well with donors and the press as it does with urban audiences is to charm people by playing the fool that they expect you to be, so that they feel less of a fool for paying you well. In this sense it seems no coincidence that Maurizio Cattelan decided to formally end his career as an artist with a Guggenheim exhibition at the very same time that Berlusconi resigned.[10] While Blairism thrives on fostering loyality, Berlusconism relies on the practical logic of jovial fraternisation. The feeling around which (temporary) working collectives form (for example, to realise a project or prepare an exhibition) is the feeling of being in on a joke together (for as long as the joke is being told and then you disband). Instiutions and audiences are happy to share this sense of being *in* on the joke, even if it is *on* them. When the artist or curator makes fun of you openly, you still feel taken seriously, because you understand what the exhibition is about. The false democracy of tricksterdom lies in the sense of community created by the shared feeling that we are all getting fooled by the same person, and we like it, because that is what we appointed him to do.

Putinism knows many forms. On the one hand it manifests itself in a particular form of institutional baroque: any venture in the art field depends on a multiplicity of people collaborating on organising it in numerous small acts of communication, such as the way an exhibition is talked into being, how funds are raised, artists involved and the public communicated with. To pretend that one person alone could actually embody this entire operation and claim it as their creation and capital is an illusion. Yet, to create this illusion and give the public the sense that they are dealing with a contemporary Louis XIV – who represents the state because he *is* the state – is what still seems to be expected from the directors of major institutions. *documenta* curatorship, for instance, almost by default, seems to demand a certain degree of Putinism. For how else could you make the public believe one curator could give you a world of art, when people should know that it is an army of helpers and contributors building this simulacrum?

The tough other side of Putinism is to be confronted by the iron law that the *robić swoje* is the norm when you work at street level in the arts. To self-organise is always a possibility. But the *pressure* to realise that possibility – and either get organised or give up your practice – might be as strong as the joy of experiencing the freedom of getting something started together with other people. How are we to face the pressure and enjoy the freedom to get organised? These are the motivational discourses we are offered: Putinism says that fighting for ourselves is our fate and the biggest fighter shall become 'Sun King'. Blairism says that it is your moral responsibility to get organised and perform to the best of your

10. Mauritzio Cattelan announced his retirement from art making following the exhibition 'Mauritzio Cattelan: All' at Guggenheim, New York, 4 November 2011 – 22 January 2012.

abilities, because the weight of the social is on your shoulders and society no longer exists to support you. Berlusconism says that it's all one big game and you should know how to side with the real players when you play it. The option Merkelism adds is: No dreams. No lies. Just work!

Can we not throw all these isms on the scrapheap of failed ideologies? This might be easier said than done, because, assuming these ideologies have already entered our thinking and shaped the expectations of funders, audiences and organisers alike, exorcising them might be an infinite task. So to be aware of the spirit in which people are motivated to take the initiative in the arts might be crucial to spot the moment when one of the ideologies rears its ugly head.

Scepticism won't save the day. But then again, why should the day be saved? To know how to battle depression at the end of the day is vital when you have exhausted yourself in the process of organising the social and sharing art and ideas with others. But what does it take to see the value of this kind of work? The more exhausting it gets, the more the desire for a redemptive experience becomes. This is where we tend to fall back on our motivational agendas and the ideologies creep in. For all the agendas analysed above do have one thing in common; they have a redemptive quality as they offer a messianic promise of success: to alleviate contemporary anxieties. If you only fight hard enough you may become a tsar; if you play it smart enough you will become the untouchable trickster; if you work for your community dedicatedly enough, you can join the club of celebrated entrepreneurs, artists and footballers. So even if, emotionally, taking this step involves quite an effort, it may still be crucial to just say 'no' to all forms of redemptive thinking. We might have to accept that there is nothing there to save the organisers. No moral reward is to be gained for shaping cultural institutions or sharing art and ideas. Sometimes it's rewarding by itself. Sometimes it's a drag. We do it because we want to. *And* because we need to. There is no easy way to resolve this contradiction.

Reclaim the Concept of Society at Large!

When we look at the big picture, we can at least see that we are not the only ones exposed to these troubles. After the slow dismantling of the welfare state, of citizens rights and support structures, more and more people everywhere are faced by the cruel alternative to – as Dylan put it – either start swimming or sink like a stone. The irony is that within the art field we may be the involuntary avant-garde, finding ourselves pioneering techniques of survival in a hardened materialist world. The practical knowledge artists have developed through centuries of struggling to invent ways of getting by, is what Blair recommends to the everyman: Be creative! Self-organise! For the state won't help you any more. So, irrespective of the fact that, practically, there may be few alternatives to self-organising, publicly, it is high time for a change of strategy. Instead of flaunting our social creativity, we might be better off reclaiming the concept of *society at large*!

To systematically void the concept of society at large has been part and parcel of the strategies of Putin, Berlusconi and Blair alike. Putin replaced the notion of society with the ideal of the Russian *people* (which he embodies). Berlusconi replaced it with the ideal of the successful *person* (which he embodies). And Blair erased it in the name of the *social* (which it is everyone's responsibility to foster). The point now would be to insist publicly that society is neither the people, nor the person, nor even the social. For producers of art and ideas this would mean to insist that we shape and represent the consciousness of society; but that we don't do this in the name of the nation and the people, because the art and thinking that informs a society are never just produced by the native inhabitants of that society. Neither do we do it in the name of this or that person. Because art and thinking reach out, across time and space, into the intimate space of the individual, yes, but also to the spaces of the many who may feel addressed. And art and thinking do so, not merely in pursuit of success, but in the hope of speaking to and for others, and hence to and for society at large.

Finally, the most difficult thing to do might be to disentangle the notion of the social from that of society at large. The crux of the political appraisal of self-organisation, in the spirit of Blairism, is that it foregrounds the dynamics of the social at the expense of an understanding of the composition of society. In a suggestively nebulous manner, the social is portrayed as a *fluid medium* that allows for the creative moulding of people's living and working conditions. Surely, this is a highly art-friendly view of social life, with high motivational potential. But we should also be aware that the fluidity of this notion made it exceptionally prone to abuse. In the last 20 years most of the moulding of the social fluidity, arguably, resulted in the improvement of interior design standards, not just in art spaces. The interiors of Starbucks franchises was equally succes fully moulded to look as if the company cared about organic products distributed according to free-trade agreements with self-organised coffee-bean farmers. And McDonald's is trying to follow suit. It promotes itself as green and socially conscientious, offering job training and so on. Still, the cruel logic of franchising is: either the contractors in charge of the particular franchise succeed in organising themselves in how to best sell the corporate food to the local customers or they loose their contract. It's hop or drop. Not least, the pleasant aesthetics of the fluidly social has helped to ease the conversion of living into working spaces. Laptops unfold next to homey coffee mugs all around you in your favourite cafe, as people labour away at organising their life and career electronically via the same social networks.

Preposterous as it may sound (but remember, *hubris* is a potent rhetorical device), I think, the position to take in the face of these developments is to stop advertising the appeal of social creativity as a competitive skill set, and instead to insist that, as artists and intellectuals we do what we do in the name of society at large. The fact that it is presently neither clear what that means nor who will potentially listen, shouldn't dissuade us. For when, after Putin, Berlusconi and Blair, there is no longer such a thing as society, it's probably up to us to reinvent it. And 'us' here potentially includes, not just producers of art and culture but potentially everyone - in healthcare, education, and menial labour - who create sociability with a sense and understanding for how they thereby bring life to society at large. This is not another attempt to pass the micro off as the macro. It really is a reminder that, after the erosion of society, when we speak, we *speak into the void of what society is not but could be*. And that when we organise, we don't just expand networks, we work towards possible societies. We do so when we produce a form of consciousness that is more than this or that knowledge which could be traded as capital (in return for credit points or something to list on your CV.) There is no way to substantiate any of those claims. But this is because the horizon in which they could be sustantiated, that of society at large, needs first of all to be opened again. And the best way to do so is to speak of it as if we are working for it. Who knows, when we self-organise, not merely to survive, but to enjoy the freedom of doing so, perhaps we actually are.

135 - 140

VARIABLES AND CONSTANTS

Juan A Gaitán

In this text I will propose that current institutional practices are an extension of some of the conceptual art practices that emerged during the 1960s. Paying particular attention to the South American context, the history of which I am most familiar with, I will outline some events that occurred in the 1960s, and trace the development of some critical attitudes that are now being proposed, or re-purposed, from the point of view of institutions and platforms for contemporary art.

Articulated from the perspective afforded by individuals' condition as citizens in the late 1960s and early 1970s, artists engaged with the immediate social and political realities through symbolic gestures, exceeding the space of the museum proper, intervening in an environmentshaped by political instability, state-sanctioned violence, and the beginning of the neoliberal era of transnational corporate interests.[1] As I see it, recently formed institutions and platforms all over the world – especially all over the Third World, excuse the misnomer – have emerged with a similar intention to provide a space where the rituals and codes of citizenship can be engaged with critically. This text is meant as a preliminary reflection on the idea that the contemporary art centre can be seen, in part, as a platform for critical citizenship.

One can hardly speak of Latin America, or any other geographical or geopolitical region, without ending up with generalisations. From the point of view of art, Latin America is not a criterion through which to understand current or former practices, nor through which one can establish cultural links between different works of art. Neither is Africa. Yet the two continents are comparable in other ways. In the ubiquitous and sometimes inauspicious presence of foreign agencies, many of which have played an active role in shaping local artistic and literary scenes (not always to negative effect). In the relative lack of commitment to culture on the part of local agencies (governments as well as private organisations). And in the precarious conditions under which cultural initiatives emerge and operate. Sometimes these factors are very present, sometimes they are only latent, but in any case they are there as something that can easily become real.

It is worth saying something about the arrival of foreign agents in Colombia, even in a cursory way, for it shows one of the lesser-known

1. Most of the artistic attitudes I am thinking of can be found in the catalogue accompanying the exhibition *Global Conceptualism*, 1999. *Global Conceptualism: Points of Origin 1950s–1980s*, was directed by project leaders Luis Camnitzer, Jane Farver, and Rachel Weiss, and organised by the Queens Museum of Art, New York.

effects that Cold War transnationalism had in Latin America. The example indicates that certain ideas were imported, as it were, by former students or associates of the Frankfurt School and other art and culture entrepreneurs, and began to circulate. These ideas now provide the framework of a revised, or even post-Marxist (meta critical) attitude in both political and philosophical thought, as well as in art.[2] It seems worth mentioning this side of the story, while leaving the door open to a slightly different periodic timeline in order to move on, for the sake of brevity, because it is here that social thought and research began to intersect with artistic and cultural production.

This 'chapter' in the cultural history of mid-twentieth-century Colombia specifically relates to a group of emigrés, mainly from Austria and Germany, who, during the flight of World War II, through bookstores and translations brought with them the philosophy of the Frankfurt School. In Colombia many of these translations appeared in a journal called *ECO: Revista de Cultura de Occidente* (Review of Western Culture). The journal not only included German authors, from Ranke and Fichte to Adorno and Horkheimer, but also some younger French ones (then young, at least) like Derrida and Foucault. It also included writings by Levi-Strauss, Brecht and Benjamin, and a host of other philosophers and writers we are very familiar with today, but who in the 1960s were largely unknown to the Spanish-speaking world. In this review one could find numerous references to the collapse of western culture (Adorno himself wrote several sentences to this effect), which was a relatively popular theme at the time – we are speaking of the Cold War – especially among left-leaning intellectuals. These texts provided the local intelligentsia with new theoretical and conceptual tools, and brought a set of new interpretations of Marxism, precisely during Marxism's most fecund time. Most of these texts were read from the point of view of curiosity, for the philosophical culture and cultural reality that they represented was at once expired and too distant from the local context. Nevertheless, they provided a philosophical framework for texts by local authors and critical appraisals

2. This narrative here is necessarily brief, in part because it needs thorough further investigation. It must therefore be said that these emigrés were not a homogeneous group. Even within the group of the already mentioned art and culture oriented ones, there were differences of political opinion that were kept mostly undisclosed in Colombia, but which surely warrant a more in-depth investigation into the arrival of enlightenment thinking and modern art in the country. Having only superficial information at hand, one can state, for instance, that there was at least one Nazi collaborator, Karl Buchholz, who seems to have been one of the first Nazi-authorized art dealers. See, for example, http://www.artnews.com/2011/11/17/momas-problematic-provenances/.

of Latin American art and culture that appeared regularly in the journal. In other words, they offered the tools of Aesthetics - mostly the Aesthetics of the German school - necessary to establish a sufficiently solid platform for launching the notion of Latin American Art.

In the artistic practices of the southern part of the western hemisphere, the idea of a 'concerned citizen' might be useful in trying to explain the spirit of the practices that emerged after the more formalist modernism of the 1950s. These practices are often referred to as Latin American Conceptualism, although it is important to note that they share neither a 'continental' concern, nor a methodology, nor do they rest on similar aesthetic precedents. For example, several of the essays in the catalogue of the 1999 exhibition *Global Conceptualism* insist, at various times, that Duchamp is to be assumed as a common reference around the world, which is a proposition that tends to reify a singular conception of history.

I wouldn't go as far as to claim that the artists who are lumped together under this category were 'concerned citizens'. Or whether they were producing work under similar criteria or according to a general programme. Yet, in the socially inclined works of the Neo-Concrete movement in Rio de Janeiro, in the anti-establishment work of artists like Luis Camnitzer and the Argentinian group Tucumán Arde (both working, within the structure of autocratic states), as well as in the anti-propaganda works of the Colombian Antonio Caro, and of many others, one gets the sense that there was a need to explore how art could invade the public sphere in order to counter the presence of liberal capitalism, or of state-sanctioned abuses towards indigenous and marginal communities, or against abusive working conditions, or the militancy with which the agrarian economy was being industrialised and driven away from the small-plot, co-operative utopia proposed by agrarian reforms. In some of these works there was also a concern with the affirmation of local cultural principles, but without resorting to the fetishist tendencies of ethnography and anthropology. The rise and dissemination of Socialist and anti-imperialist sentiments, of Dependency Theory, or Liberation Theology, and of Maoism also helped shape a certain solidarity (one could not call it more than that) with a range of peoples and cultures that hitherto had been either ignored or fetishised into some nationalist aesthetic programme (indigenous and black communities, as well as peasants). In the art of the 1960s and 1970s (I should emphasise here that we are speaking of only a few countries: Colombia, Venezuela, Peru,

Brazil, Argentina, Chile, Uruguay) there was also a tendency to explore how art could mobilise the citizenry, producing statements that would raise consciousness against local regimes, or against the surrendering of the national wealth to foreign interests, or against the ideological transformation (Americanisation) of local culture. Important to note here is that these practices were not only anti-institutional, but also extra-institutional, meaning that they were more concerned with their existence in the expanded field of social and political life than with their relationship, or lack thereof, with cultural institutions. They had no home, and having no home was a way of belonging in the streets, in the country, in places where culture lived rather than in places where culture *rested*.

I mention all this to expand on a point that is far simpler than the history of the practices that I have outlined above: it occurs to me that today, both in Africa and in Central and South America, and in other parts of the world, platforms and institutions have emerged with the intention of intervening in, or disrupting the logic of the everyday, in terms of political and social consciousness, by way of the support of a critical engagement with culture. In other words, these are places that are formed in order to allow space for a different relationship with contemporary cultural practices, and that recognise that an institutional setup may facilitate access to certain kinds of thinking (let's say, artistic thinking) that would otherwise be inaccessible. But they are also places that hope to promote, through art, a differential relationship to the immediate environment by accessing a more global source of cultural practice. One might call these 'platforms for comparative citizenship'. Platforms on which citizens of one place are able to recognise patterns and realities that are perhaps distant but that resonate with their own; but also on which certain gestures (from simple ones, like the open-door policy that many follow, to more complicated ones, like the reshuffling of the relationships between private, artistic and political life) can give audiences new ideas on how to relate to the political and social realities of everyday life. Where globalisation itself might be recognised, both in its financial and political power, but also with its cultural limits.

These institutions hope to emerge and remain, against adversity and against the financial odds, in order to embody the notion that the relationship between cultural institutions and its audience does not need to be as programmatic as it tends to be when it is in the hands of government or foreign agencies. In many places, there seems to be an ambition nowadays to re-educate the agencies that fund culture locally, to make them recognise that the guidelines for their funding applications tend to enforce a certain idea of what culture is and how it is to be managed, when in fact the point is that culture should not be managed at all. If there is one zone in which one should allow a society, and the different groups within it, to follow its own collective intuition, it is the zone of culture. And I use the word 'intuition' with a purpose: not in order to propose an uncritical production or reproduction of cultural capital, but in order to suggest a method which resists programmatic terms of behaviour and production, and that opens up a multiplicity of directions of critical and analytical approaches to cultural production, taking into account the social, political and economic realities that affect it.

Perhaps with some idealism - which I consider necessary today - certain gestures (from the open-door policy, to the inclusion of sophisticated forms of critical thought) allow citizens to enter the space of culture from a more active perspective. It is exactly there that the potential for a critical relationship that folds back into the spaces of citizenship resides. Perhaps it folds back merely in the form of an expectation - the expectation (even if it necessarily stays at the level of expectation) that access to culture should be free, for instance - or perhaps it folds back into it in the form of a commitment. Either way, if contemporary art oscillates critically between the formal and the political, it is because form is a sign of an institutionalisation of culture that stands in need of expansion in order to include the notion of culture at large, an active culture, not exclusively drawn to traditional, museum-oriented pictorial or compositional notions. In this sense, these places or spaces that I would like to refer to as 'platforms for comparative citizenship' are there merely as formal propositions for approaching culture in relation to the social and political conditions that most directly affect the spaces of cultural production and circulation, at least for now.

WHAT MORE DO YOU WANT THAN FREEDOM?

Charles Esche interviewed by Ekaterina Degot & David Riff

EKATERINA DEGOT Today, art institutions, and not just in western Europe, seem to be challenged from two sides. Some blame them of ignoring their social engagement and only cultivating pure art for the educated few, while others would claim exactly the opposite: museums like the Van Abbemuseum are too socially engaged, in the sense that they produce nothing but social relations. In the Russian context, many would agree with the second position. The way art functions in late social democracy reminds them of the late Soviet art system, which, in theory, was to bring socially relevant art to mass audiences, and wound up being primitively didactic, infantilising and tendentious. The claim is that western institutions do not see the dangers that this model implies.

CHARLES ESCHE Well, I find myself disagreeing with both sides in different ways. Perhaps I have less sympathy for the critics of social engagement, but it is true that there is a real danger of art's instrumentalisation by politics or economics – two competing value systems that can each destroy art's capacity to imagine the world otherwise. However, I think the threat of instrumentalisation comes more from market fundamentalism than from whatever we might call late social democracy.

If I refer to the Van Abbemuseum, we are basically a product of high social democracy and have been complicit with its survival as an ideology since 1945. So, it is not so surprising that, as an institution, the museum reflects the confused goals or compromised values of the slow collapse of functioning social democracy. Indeed, I have so little sense of a social democratic agenda in the Netherlands today that I don't think it exists anymore as a coherent idea of society, beyond a rear-guard defence of the welfare state. Yet, as a public institution, the museum is still its product and therefore carries its failure inside it.

In my western European experience I am not so sure that the two critical voices you characterise in your question are really so very different. I can characterise them as conservative and neoliberal, and both are, for me, products of this collapse of a dynamic social democratic ideology that previously linked artistic thinking and aesthetic knowledge to a quality of citizenship. From this general condition, your two critics are apparently quite opposite while both are reacting to the same situation by effectively trying to marginalise a critical, contemporary voice.

The conservative side are generally those with a vestigial sympathy for high social democracy, sometimes even members of the rump party itself. They are often aesthetically conservative in the sense that they see art in terms of the 1970s split between New York school minimalism and German expressive figuration. That battle was a radical adjustment for westerners of the post-1945 generation, and somehow they cannot see past it. They are essentially nostalgic for the certainties of the Cold War, for 1968 and all that, while wanting art to retain its autonomy in the old sense of being a demonstration of 'western freedom' in the face of communist instrumentalisation. They haven't adjusted to the post-1989 landscape, and in some ways remind me of the lost generation after the end of Communism in that they don't quite seem to understand that something major changed in their environment. These people are a big element of the opposition to our programme at the museum, as you might expect, and are generally opposed to a renewal of the social mission of cultural institutions.

On the neo-liberal side, there is a simple demand for art to serve the economy. Publicly funded cultural institutions are simply not part of their worldview, and if art doesn't make money it should only be a private concern. If they have any opinion about art at all, then they probably would see it as providing appropriate decorations for the financialised system of capital accumulation. For neo-liberals, anything that would encourage collective expression or offer alternative subjectivities of what it is to be public – especially if reliant on the public purse – must be marginalised, as that threatens the holy image of the market as the only provider of innovation or personal satisfaction. Their accusations may be that the Van Abbemuseum is too didactic or tendentious, but, if you go further, it is the message they disapprove of more than the means. The collective is the neo-liberal bête noire and I think they might genuinely believe that any expression of social collectivity is dangerous. In doing so, they instrumentalise art in the service of the free market.

ED To clarify what I mean by a conservative position is that it is often being voiced by former conceptualists and their followers, who are neither for purely decorative art, nor for anti-avantgarde aesthetics. They are into didactic and often narrative art in a way themselves, but based on experiences under state socialism, they do not believe in art institutions as such, neither do they believe in wider audiences for art other than imagined audiences, an art project in itself.

CE OK. Then the situation in Russia is slightly different. The demand for a wide audience for art is sacrosanct in western arguments, both from the old social democrats who want the people to 'see' their kind of western art out of political-ideological motivations, and from the neo-liberals who want museums to make money out of ticket sales. In many ways, I am sympathetic to a critique of our museum that would ask us to exhibit more artistic freedom and less political education or market efficiency. I just don't often get the question! Maybe its origin has more to do with the uses of art in the Soviet Union. As I understand it, the consequence of Soviet policy was the instrumentalisation of the arts to the degree that there was no critical possibility anymore. Of course, this is problematic to say the least, but I also admit to appreciating the aesthetic appeal of socialist realism. Those paintings are uplifting – seeing Stalin greeting the wives of the factory workers, or the glorious light in that famous *Letter from the Front* painting in the Tretyakov. They do lift your spirits, and you can imagine why it was necessary in a society that was going through existential threats from its own experiments and from foreign invasion.

ED What you say is true, especially if you mean bigger names, but the Soviet art system produced thousands of almost identical images of workers without any particular value in terms of form or content. Ultimately, it produced extreme redundancy and few great artists. Of course, the very idea of 'greatness' was in a way considered undemocratic. And of course, from this Soviet point of view, western modernist art also looks almost all identical and boring... But the most productive reception of socialist realist paintings concerned their amusing emptiness, the void of the language, which inspired the Moscow conceptualists in the 1970s.

CE We can probably agree that Soviet Communism as a potent, reformative force died around 1968, and that its art followed a similar trajectory. Maybe it sounds a bit superficial to say this now, but I think Soviet artists were struggling with what to do when the good guys are in charge. Of course, one answer is to wait until they become bad guys, but there is a genuine issue here that also impacts on artists under social democratic systems. From people like Rodchenko and Lissitzky onwards, the question of how to praise and yet remain independent was a hard one. Social democracy resolved it temporarily through the idea of pure artistic autonomy, even if it was always regulated through a bureaucratic system - but this floundered from the 1980s neo-liberal revolution onwards. Soviet systems were different and that maybe opened up an ironic or amused space, as you say. But both systems are now in the past, though a country like the Netherlands has difficulty realising this.

What is more pertinent here, when we think about issues of critical artistic thinking today, is how two centuries of human effort to create a more equal, more just society have apparently been abandoned entirely in the last twenty years. Modern art and modernist aesthetic experiments were part of this effort, and their loss is traumatic for artistic practice today. The reason for this abandonment of ambition - of imagination even - is closely tied to the neo-liberal narrative of the failure of communism, and that's why it is difficult for somebody with a western European upbringing like me to fully abandon any redeeming features in even post-1960s real existing Communism. It is maybe why the years of Brezhnev stagnation are interesting for me today. However, I'm willing to admit to lack of rigour here, brought on by a desire to think beyond the western *Denkverbot* in a place of rigid consensus like the Netherlands. What I want to ensure is that art in 2013 can claim a role in not only critically addressing social conditions, but in expressing and modelling collectivities, and in shaping the imagination of the world as it could be and not only as it is. The idea that this was tried before and failed, and that therefore we should abandon it completely, seems utterly pessimistic. By the way, it also undermines any basis whatsoever for having public spaces for contemporary art, as art is no longer associated with any public goal.

ED There is also an illusion of the role of art in this criticism; that art becomes purely defined by its content. It is never said openly, but every artist knows that the politics of smaller, so-called progressive institutions are to support projects according to relevance of their topic, almost exclusively. Issues of form are considered too debatable, too narrowly professional.

CE That's probably a legitimate critique. I know institutions where the modes of display look tired, or unconsidered, while they claim a certain radical agenda. I hope the Van Abbemuseum is not one of them! Certainly our experiments with collection exhibitions and forms of public interaction have been very deliberately concerned with the form of the museum, its displays and how the work is 'shown'. I also know small institutions where the exhibition and the interaction with the public, the 'work of art' if you like, seem less important than the debate – but I don't think that's too severe a crime.

In general, I do think art is quite robust and can defend itself from clumsy attempts to instrumentalise it in exhibitions. What I see as more vulnerable at this point are the public platforms at which a public encounter with art can take place. I want to defend this artistic space as one that has its own rights and responsibilities, distinct from a political platform or an economic asset. Justifying its right to exist on the basis of secondary aspects such as tourism, local regeneration or social inclusion will be fatal in the long term. The artistic space I want to defend is associated with a certain way of thinking, in which certain personal and social values can be expressed that I think are absolutely imperative to sustain a balanced and emancipated society. This artistic thinking is equally vital for democratic exchange, as one of the ways in which we can project our subjectivity and find empathy for the ideas of others. This is the job of the public institution, and I am convinced it needs to be maintained in the public interest.

Coming from western Europe, I cannot avoid relating this thinking to autonomy. In the Netherlands, students are taught autonomous art and they have established a tradition where autonomy is a given, rather than something taken by an artist shaping their own form of agency. The partially good intentions behind this development have resulted to my mind in a disabling of art's capacity to affect society. The handing out of autonomy by a superior power means that art has been given a priori right to be tolerated, provided it has no unwanted consequences for that power itself. While social democracy was confident in its toleration, those limits were quite generous, but they were always there.

If you compare it with the Soviet experience, with its nominally extreme politicisation, we have a kind of extreme 'autonomitisation' sanctioned by the state, and in which you can only apply your autonomy to the field of art itself. Stepping outside these boundaries, seeking connections with social forms and contexts is seen as an ungrateful response. 'What more do you want than freedom?', the social democrats may ask you. Neo-liberals will see socially engaged art as a sort of interference with the private sphere of political, social or lifestyle choices. Of course, once power is in their hands, the consequences of an autonomy that is given are much clearer and the space to act is further restricted by subsidy cuts and privatisation. Yet, I still despise this current Dutch government because of its rhetoric rather than its cuts. When the Under-Minister of Culture says that art is only a private interest he chooses to deny any critical, reflective, social or public role for art, and largely gets away with it in the media and among my colleagues.

DAVID RIFF I think Ekaterina makes an interesting point. The institutional art world fosters tendentiousness, which covers up political and aesthetic apathy. This seems a general attribute of the crumbling state ideological apparatus (incompletely transformed and essentially broken through shock therapy, through neo-liberalism, itself now in crisis). Crisis brings about so many autonomitisation effects: it's every man (or every clan) for himself. Under the Brezhnev stagnation, there was a remarkable withdrawal, or interiorisation, to safe communal autonomy zones beyond the institutions, and there were many such interstices where self-organisation was possible in a nearly utopian mode of art making. One key difference is that the late Brezhnevian institutional world was essentially closed off to experimental practices, if they weren't purely formal or decorative, while today's apparatus welcomes them, especially if they are politically engaged and aesthetically experimental. This opens a whole new can of worms, of course, because we can talk about the decline of social democracy and its reinvigoration or rebranding through the appropriation of more radical energies, which then become part of the apparatus themselves.

CE This is a really pertinent critique and one I am aware of without having a good answer. The issue is perhaps clearest in Israel, where so-called 'leftist' cultural institutions are funded by a state that still claims to be the 'only democracy in the Middle East' while denying basic rights to people under its rule. Part of that claim is based on the space those Israeli cultural institutions are given to be critical, and they are therefore made complicit with the repressive actions of the state. Much the same is true in other western countries, where art is a part of the apparatus of state management. I can see the Van Abbemuseum as a part of the argument for proclaiming Dutch tolerance internationally while not recognising the crimes of its military or its corporations throughout the world. I suppose my answer up to now has always been that the western state is reformable, and that art and its institutions can be part of constructing an emancipatory movement from within liberal democracy. Since the 2008 financial crisis and the ensuing neo-liberal austerity, it has become harder to maintain that stance. I do see that both conservative and neo-liberal criticisms of the Van Abbemuseum are getting more vocal, and that gives me some encouragement that we are not only an alibi for the state. Neo-liberals and social democrats have turned inwards, wanting to isolate art more as they focus on protecting their safe western European home. Our forms of internationalism in the museum annoy them and stir them a little from their apathy, but our museum does not (yet) stir people into action. Perhaps that might be something to come, but by then we could no longer expect the kind of public subsidy we currently enjoy.

Your comment about the Brezhnev stagnation interests me a lot. I don't think our current situation in western Europe is so different from those days. We have the meaningless repetition of capitalist pieties, the empty rhetoric of the free market, a relatively large part of our democratic system is only theatrical and there is a class of capitalist bureaucrats (the politicians, corporate CEOs etc.) that is increasingly separated from the rest of society while making decisions apparently on its behalf. These are quite similar conditions to the Soviet Union of the 1970s, as I understand it. We have a tendency towards oligarchy everywhere in Europe, something that is essentially a stagnant form of government. The issue is how to respond. A similar active resignation to the 1970s, a sort of neo-refusenik action, might be valid. I am tempted by such a withdrawal, because the capacity for innovation, for thinking differently – which is a capacity of art – is severely limited in this situation. But I am swithering still, not yet fully convinced of retreat as a strategy, however appealing it is personally.

DF What seems so eerie is that today's art world reproduces the oligarchal-feudal-stagnant model you describe, but it also produces a new form of agency, the freelance 'innovator', whose job it can be to reform or reoccupy the increasingly defunct, neglected autonomy zone, to bring something from outside. Neo-liberalism has meant, among other things, the institutionalisation of this figure. Yesterday's activists and self-organisers become tomorrow's flexible apparatchiks, busy constructing what is essentially a cultural alibi. Former activists and artistic experimenters become poster children for neo-liberalism at its most humane...

CE I think we have to be careful here. I'm not sure we can throw out all forms of activism as adverts for neo-liberalist flexibility and dynamism. There is real conflict still, and it also does happen in the art world. We could do with more clarity, but the interesting thing I see happening at the moment is the emergence of a split in the art world in which commercial and non-commercial sectors are separating in terms of publics, discourses and critical appraisal. You are right in saying that this split is not clear, and that the activist can still be turned into an agent of neo-liberalism, but I think the gap is getting wider and more defined. This has also to do with the hardening of neo-liberalism that accompanies its austerity regime. I'm quite wary of the sufficiency of criticality alone at the moment. I think we may need to align our institutions more with campaigns for justice and become directly engaged in particular local issues that reveal the contradictions of a neo-liberal agenda. This is not happening enough at the moment, and I feel personally late in realising how vital this now is. I agree that it makes artistic actions vulnerable to co-option by politics, but I think at the local level it might be possible. In the end it is a question of how viable a critical museum is today.

We need to construct a new political imagination and I think that art and its public institutions have a role in that. It is partly the role of trying to divert whatever excesses are being produced by the system for other means. This is fragile and temporary, but I am still convinced of its necessity despite my doubts about the critical museum's viability in neo-liberal times. If we can get hold of these excesses to construct another imagination, that will be worthwhile. And I think in my wildest dreams that is what we are trying to provide in Eindhoven when we re-imagine the museum, examine its collection and rewrite its histories. Given the fact that the institution owns a tiny part of the past, we can try to write the past in order to change the future.

DF How far back should this rewriting and re-imagining go? Should it primarily be concerned with reclaiming a twentieth-century modernist legacy? Or maybe we need to address the notions and form that arose during the Enlightenment, and even before, in an earlier modernity?

CE All the way. The year 1848 is a key date for me at the moment. To be specific in terms of the museum, the models that we're looking at include early anatomy museums, the Sir John Soane Museum in London, John Ruskin's Mechanics Institutes, the Kupferstichkabinett in Berlin, the early history of the Rijksmuseum in Amsterdam. These were all responses to the Enlightenment and industrialisation. What we're trying to do is develop an idea of the collection as a static display while the lines of approach and the narratives that run through that display are multiple and constantly in flux. The idea is to create an institution that would be rather more like a non-lending library than a museum. This would shift the curatorial and artistic address from the spatial arrangement of objects to the narratives that are told by highlighting certain of those objects through guides, media systems and located discussions. The task shifts to an arrangement of voice and narration. This seems to me to open up new possibilities for the act of curating. It is no longer about collecting or promoting names or isolated, precious objects, but about thinking through the stories that need to be told to different kinds of people and who tells them. Hopefully you can involve artists, architects, politicians, cleaners and the wider public in that process. If we succeed, we can alter the hierarchy of who can tell those stories and exchange with people from outside the curatorial cadre.

The other advantage is that you will free up time and resources to develop what I call the 'dispersed museum'. This is the idea that the museum itself only has a small percentage of its activities within its four walls, and disperses its knowledge to people outside, in Ramallah, in rural China, in a small suburb of Eindhoven. Even modernist classics like Picasso have something to contribute here, once you release them from the straightjacket of formalist art history.

DF I have a small pragmatic question: how difficult is it to actually do these things? I'm sure it's not easy to work in the Netherlands with a right-wing populist government and the dire situation of extreme cuts. What kind of conflicts have you encountered? What are the expectations of your bureaucratic constituency on the one hand, and what are the expectations of your audience on the other?

CE The core problem we are facing in the museum is a loss of legitimacy for our historical position. The state is no longer able to maintain the institutions it created for itself in the 1945 to 1989 period. This inevitably brings the future of the museum into question. As I said, both rump social democrats and neo-liberals have reasons to be unhappy with art and with us as a museum. Populists are of course only concerned with anything as a means to power. Together they make it an unfriendly environment in which to direct a museum. Locally in Eindhoven there is also quite a strong pragmatic drive towards design as a future identity for this post-industrial city. Art doesn't have much traction there because we are looking at arguments for economic survival in a non-touristic place. A critical culture is not encouraged. So, it is tough at that level.

On the other hand, the financial cuts themselves are part of a timely global re-balancing. The old, imperial states finally have to give ground to the rest, and we can expect many cultural institutions to close. Each institutional death is a small, individual tragedy of course, but I doubt the sum total of Dutch society's attention to culture will change that much. It might have a positive effect on some people, by provoking them to value the surviving institutions more than they do now.

This situation also gives us as a cultural field an opportunity to reform, even as we have less money from the state. Priorities become more crucial: we have a chance to do things that were traditionally forbidden. To develop the initiatives I spoke about, I want to try and divert money from the remaining excess of capitalism held by the oligarchic class, while keeping our current objectives and maintaining our space for artistic thinking. I am not sure that is going to be easy, but neither is negotiating with the state these days. At least we are more likely to find sympathetic ears among some maverick oligarchs. Ideally, I would like to negotiate a path between what remains of the public sector and private wealth, playing one off against the other if I can.

DF Have you already worked in such public-private partnerships?

CE We had an exhibition called *The Collectors Show* in 2011 that brought in the local collectors by showing a few works from their collections. It was an attempt to be more transparent about the relationships that allow the museum to flourish. We wanted to put a focus on the collectors themselves by interviewing them and showing videos of their relationship to art, the public and the museum alongside the works in their collections. I hope it will have an effect in the longer term.

DF Over the last years, Russia has been a testing ground for a very radical version of what you describe. From top to bottom, contemporary art is bankrolled by lesser and greater oligarchs. That has meant a vast proliferation of vanity culture, since many artists cater to an imaginary demand from glossy lifestyle art. 'Re-imagining' the museum, or artistic practice, or curating, in this case means its wholesale privatisation, to the point of the state mimicking oligarchical values and glamorous culture too. So even a municipal or federal state art institution runs the danger of becoming a vanity project based exclusively on personal interest and personal taste imposed by personal financing. It is very difficult in practice to negotiate between these different vanity projects to make something substantial, and even more difficult – at least until now – to reveal economic structures or hidden agendas. Maybe the future of Europe looks like this too, once social democracy is dismantled completely?

CE Maybe, yes. The collapse of social democracy is happening too slowly for many of the oligarchic class, and this is partly why there's interest in promoting an even bigger economic crisis. They can then unmake the whole welfare state – though of course there are risks to them as well. If you don't have that space I am trying to find to negotiate between public and private, it will certainly be more difficult. Then you have to play one oligarch off against another. And through that combination, you can perhaps construct some sort of space of relative autonomy. As long as they don't make such overwhelming demands for control that your own agency is reduced to nothing...

ED But I think even if they don't do that, at least in Russia, the curator reacts as if they would.

CE But that's what I mean. Do we really push the oligarch enough? Do we really take a position, as a curatorial or artistic field, saying 'these are our demands and these are our requirements? Are you prepared to fund it?' I would still be interested to see to what extent you can negotiate the relationship between oligarch and citizen. Is there a way in which you can create a moment of consciousness of the relationship with sponsorship? So that the sponsors can be put in the spotlight, which is what they want, at the same time as their influence can be quietly considered by the public. I would be interested in those negotiations, if only because my experience of state sponsored control is problematic, especially in recent days.

DR How much hope should one place in the more depersonalised corporate sponsorship and its institutional critique? How much of that is a legitimisation of corporate policy through criticality displays? And how much can one actually influence corporations through art? Is that even an option?

CE Personally, I would have much less trust in corporations than individual oligarchs. They are both less subject to quixotic opinions and enthusiasms, and also less socially responsible, in that they can preach the doctrine of the indifferent invisible hand to foreswear any ethical position. Socially, the corporations are much more the enemy than individual oligarchs. They produce injustice systematically. I am sure art is never going to be effective in changing corporate strategies, while it might change an individual of whatever wealth. It is art's job to challenge the social perception of the corporations, change the way a citizen looks at them and their activities. So I don't think we are completely powerless, but it's a slow process that involves artistic action alongside street protests, collective organisation, net activism etc. The heart of the problem lies in the lack of social imagination within the political field to see beyond corporate capital and its attractions. This is essentially the political tragedy of our age – to be living at a time of cluelessness in relation to the future.

DF Before you talked about the possibility of total collapse, massive expropriation, disenfranchisement, and radical exclusion. Will this really unleash an outburst of imagination?

CE You want a prediction? OK, here goes. The first thing to say is that living will become harder. We are going to lose cash, security, mobility – so it's not a great prospect if you value your current lifestyle. But yes, the imaginative capacity of humanity will increase, while its productive and economic capacity will decrease. I'm sure that will happen. The second thing is that the challenge will be to maintain our networks and keep international discussion going. We must avoid becoming localists. Maybe we need to think in terms of the communication between universities in the twelfth-century renaissance – small enclaves here and there that discuss and make a difference. We'll have the advantage of being on the side of history again as our critique of capitalism will be vindicated.

Things will become possible that seem impossible now too. The whole question of the complicity of institutions will be irrelevant. We'll use whatever we can use for however long we can use it. Simple.

But the moment capitalism stops working for the 1%, and that means stops giving them 10-15% increase in wealth every 12 months – then their interest will no longer be in maintaining the free market. So we can imagine a return to protectionism and retreat to nation-state solutions accelerating. Fascism will be a danger as the citizenry become alienated. The oligarchies will fail to see that alienation and at some point citizens will revolt. It has happened in the past, it can happen again. However unimaginable it is. And the question then is what side the citizens will choose and how they will be able to express themselves. Here, I hope the dreams of the net activists and the little social models in art can play a real role. That's why it is worth to keep artistic thinking going, right up to the moment this all happens.

Biographies

Julie Ault

Julie Ault is an artist, curator, writer, and editor who works both independently and collaboratively. She often assumes curatorial and editorial roles as forms of artistic practice. In 1979 Ault co-founded Group Material, whose practice explored the relationship between art, activism, and politics until disbanding in 1996. Ault's recent exhibitions include: 'Ever Ephermal, Remembering and Forgetting in the Archive', Signal, Malmö, 2011, and 'No-Stop City High-Rise: a conceptual equation', with Martin Beck, for the São Paulo Bienal, 2010. Her edited and authored publications include: (FC) *Two Cabins* by James Benning (2011), *Show and Tell: A Chronicle of Group Material* (2010), and *Come Alive! The Spirited Art of Sister Corita* (2006).

David Blamey

David Blamey is a London-based artist, occasional curator and writer, proprietor of independent publishing imprint Open Editions and editor of the Occasional Table anthology series. Recent projects include: 'O.K.' released in the Voice Studies series by My Dance the Skull (2013); 'Quite Place' curated exhibition for *Electric Spring*, Huddersfield (2013); and 'Craked, White, Open', Jochen Hempel Gallery, Berlin (2012).

Maibritt Borgen

Maibritt Borgen is a freelance curator and art historian currently pursuing a Ph.D in Art History at Yale University, New Haven, CT. She was Helena Rubinstein Critical Studies Fellow at the Whitney Independent Study Program (2010-2011), and project director of Osloo at the Venice Biennale (2011). Furthermore, she held the position as vice chairwoman and board member of the Young Art Workers in Denmark from 2009 to 2010.

Céline Condorelli

Céline Condorelli is an artist and author, currently working as professor at Nuova Accademia Di Belle Arti, Milan. Her recent works have been included in exhibitions such as *Surrounded by the Uninhabitable*, SALT Istanbul (2011-2012) and *Manifesta 8-OVERSCORE* in Murcia (2010). Condorelli is the author/editor of *Support Structures* (Sternberg Press, 2009) and one of the founding directors of Eastside Projects, an artist-run exhibition space in Birmingham, England.

Anthony Davies, Stephan Dillemuth & Jakob Jakobsen

After running a Contemporary Art and Dance project space in Cologne in the early 80s, Jakob Jakobsen went to Italy on a state funded study trip, where he met Stephan Dillemuth who was working as a temp at the local post office during the day and ran a vegetarian juice bar (E.g.g. Bar) together with his wife Anthony Davies, at night. After an acrimonious divorce, Davies joined the Royal Navy and, along with Jakobsen (at the time a flight attendant on EasyJet), saw action in the first Gulf War. Dillemuth however went to Nepal for self-realisation.

Coincidentally, all three met again years later in Copenhagen, where Davies gained a part-time teaching post on Critical Sound Art an the Royal Academy of Art and Design. Together they published their first text, TINA1, in 1985.

Ekaterina Degot

Ekaterina Degot is an essayist and freelance curator. Her solo- and co-curated projects include, among others, 'Art After the End of the World', discussion platform of the 1st Kiev Biennial (2012); the 1st Ural Industrial Biennial (Ekaterinburg, 2010); Auditorium Moscow (Moscow, 2011); Soviet Art Between Trotzky and Stalin, New Manege (Moscow, 2008). Together with David Riff she convenes the Bergen Assembly, Bergen in 2013. She lives and works in Moscow.

Barnaby Drabble

Barnaby Drabble is an independent curator, writer and researcher based in Zürich, Switzerland. His work focuses on social and political issues in contemporary art, including the use of public-space, urbanism, migration, intellectual property and civil disobedience. He lectures on contemporary art and curating at the Postgraduate Programme in Curating at Zürich University of the Arts, which he co-founded in 2005. He is also a member of the faculty of the Master of Arts in Public Spheres at l'Ecole cantonale d'art du Valais, Sierre, Switzerland. In addition, he is also managing editor of the Journal for Artistic Research and writes for international art press, catalogues and publications. With Dorothy Richter, he developed the Curating Degree Zero Archive in 2003 and has published two anthologies of text on curating.

Jonas Ekeberg

Jonas Ekeberg trained as an artist and has been active as a curator and critic since the early nineties. He is editor of the Nordic online journal Kunstkritikk. He has served as the director of Preus Museum, the national museum for photography in Norway (2004-2009). He was the chief curator of Momentum – The Nordic biennial for contemporary art in 2000. Subsequently, he was a curator at the Office for Contemporary Art Norway from 2002 to 2004. Throughout his career he has lectured and published widely. Ekeberg is currently working on a book about the rise and fall of the Nordic art scene in the period 1990–2010.

Linus Elmes

Linus Elmes is an artist, writer and curator, currently director at UKS (Young Artists Society) in Oslo, Norway. Elmes has a background in Swedish artist initiated projects such as ak28 (2003-2007) and Ersta Konsthall (2006-2009) and have curated a number of exhibitions with artists such as BHQF and Atelier Van Lieshout. He recently published *No Gods, No Parents*; an Encyclopaedia of para-textual material such as manifestos, legal and financial statements, memoirs, proposals, formal requests and letters of intent from a particular field within contemporary art recognised under many names – the alternative, artist-run and the self-organised scene maybe among the most common.

Charles Esche

Charles Esche is a curator and writer. He is director of Van Abbemuseum, Eindhoven, the Netherlands and co-director of Afterall

Journal and Books based at Central St. Martins College of Art and Design, London, England. He has curated the 5th U3 triennial in Ljubljana, Slovenia (2010), the 3rd Riwaq Biennale together with Reem Fadda (Ramallah, Palestine, 2009) and the 9th Istanbul Biennale with Vasif Kortun (2005). From 2000 to 2004 he was the director of the Rooseum Center for Contemporary Art, Malmö. He has written for several art magazines including Artforum, Frieze, Parkett and Art Monthly. A book of his selected writings, *Modest Proposals*, was published by Baglam Press, Istanbul in 2005.

Juan A Gaitán

Juan A Gaitán is a curator and writer, currently based in Mexico City. His previous curatorial projects include *The End of Money* (Witte de With, 2011), *Models for Taking Part*, which started in Vancouver, Canada in early 2011, at Presentation House Gallery, and has toured to two other institutions since, and *K* (CCA-Wattis in San Francisco, 2012). He has written for *The Exhibitionist*, *Afterall*, *Mousee*, and *Fillip*, among other publications dedicated to contemporary art. Until June of 2012 he was adjunct professor at the California College for the Arts. He is currently curator of the 8th Berlin Biennale for Contemporary Art.

Johan Frederik Hartle

Johan Frederik Hartle is assistant professor for philosophy of art and culture at the University of Amsterdam (UvA). He has taught at several international art schools including the Rietveld Academy, Amsterdam, the Academy of Fine Arts, Münster and the China Academy of Art, Hangzhou. Hartle's research focuses on the aesthetico-political, the aftermath of Marxism and institutional theories of art. Most recent book publications are *Der geöffnete Raum. Zur Politik der ästhetischen Form* (Munich, 2006) and *Personal Kill* (with Beate Geissler and Oliver Sann, Nuremberg, 2011). His published work furthermore includes catalogue essays on Rainer Ganahl, Leopold Kessler, and Michael Sailstorfer.

Stine Hebert

Stine Hebert is a curator and art historian based in Copenhagen, Denmark. Hebert has practiced as a freelance curator for a number of years focusing on investigations of conditions for artistic production. She co-founded the initiative AUX - forum for sound and has produced exhibitions for various spaces internationally and lectured at universities and art academies in the Nordic countries. Hebert was previously Acting Director of BAC - Baltic Art Center in Sweden and curator at Kunsthal Charlottenborg in Copenhagen, and has recently been appointed Rector of Funen Art Academy in Denmark.

Abdellah Karroum

Abdellah Karroum is an independent curator and researcher, based in Morocco. He founded L'appartement 22 in Rabat in 2002, and has developed numerous projects including Editions Hors'champs in Bordeaux, and artistic expeditions Le Bout Du Monde (Rif and elsewhere). He has served as curator for the DAK'ART Biennial for African Contemporary Art (2006), Gwangju Biennale (2008), and Marrakech Biennale (2009). He curated 'Working for Change', a Proposal for a Moroccan Pavilion at the 54th Venice Biennale 2011, was the co-curator of 'Intense Proximity', the 3rd edition of La Triennale at Palais de

Tokyo in Paris (2012) and artistic director of Biennale Bénin 2012 'Inventer le Monde : l'Artiste Citoyen'.

Livia Pancu

Livia Pancu is based in Iaşi, Romania. Since 2005 she worked for three years in different positions, in many projects run by Vector such as: cARTier (2004 - 2007), Backyard Residency - New Program of Artists' Residences in South-East Europe (2007 - 2008), Periferic 7 - Focussing Iaşi (2006). From 2005 she was a member of Vector Association, from 2011 to 2012 also its director. She is currently co-director at tranzit.ro, part of the international network tranzit.org. Projects recently organised and co-curated: 'I am working, I am producing, I am controlling' at Zona Gallery, Lodz, Poland (2011), 'Vector Association at Western Front' co-curated with Jesse McKee at Western Front, Vancouver, Canada (2011), 'Critical Point', Vector's participation in Frieze Projects, London (2010), *Ulu - Contemporary Art*, Iaşi, Romania, part of the exhibition Friends of the Divided Mind, Royal College of Art, London (2009) co-curated with Preeti Khaturia and Jesse McKee. Livia Pancu is interested in understanding the different internal mechanics of contemporary art organisations (almost institutions) in non-capital cities.

David Riff

David Riff is a writer, artist, and curator who teaches at the Rodchenko School for Photography and Multimedia in Moscow. A member of the group Chto delat?, he co-edited the newspaper of the same name from 2003 to 2008 contributing numerous articles to this and other publications. Artistic collaborations include the Karl Marx School of the English Language (together with Dmitry Gutov), which contributed audio-painting-installations to the 52nd Venice Biennial (2005) and the group exhibition The Potosi Principle (Madrid-Berlin-La Paz, 2010-11). Major curatorial projects include the 1st Ural Industrial Biennial Shockworkers of the Mobile Image (with Ekaterina Degot and Cosmin Costinas, 2010) and Auditorium Moscow (with Ekaterina Degot and Joanna Mytkowska, 2011): a month-long program of discussions, screenings, and workshops. He is currently one of two conveners of the Bergen Assembly 2013.

Anne Szefer Karlsen

Anne Szefer Karlsen is a curator and writer, currently Director of Hordaland Art Centre in Bergen, Norway. In addition to series of exhibitions and seminars for the Hordaland Art Centre, as well as further developing its residency programme, she has curated exhibitions for other art spaces, such as Bergen Art Museum, L'appartement 22 and Oslo Fine Art Society. She is co-founder of Ctrl+Z Publishing for which she co-edited *Lokalisert/Localised* with Arne Skaug Olsen and Morten Kvamme (Ctrl+Z Publishing, 2009). Szefer Karlsen was Associate Curator of Biennale Bénin 2012 'Inventer le Monde : l'Artiste Citoyen (Artistic director Abdellah Karroum) and is curator for Lofoten International Art Festival - LIAF 2013 'Just what is it that makes today so familiar, so uneasy?' (with Bassam El Baroni and Eva González-Sancho).

Jan Verwoert

Jan Verwoert is a critic and writer on contemporary art and cultural theory, based in Berlin, Germany. He is a contributing editor of *frieze* magazine. He teaches at the Piet Zwart Institute in Rotterdam, the de Appel curatorial programme in Amsterdam (both in the Netherlands), the Ha'Midrasha School of Art, Tel Aviv, Israel and the Bergen Academy of Art and Design, Norway. Verwoert is the author of *Bas Jan Ader: In Search of the Miraculous* (MIT Press/Afterall Books, 2006) and the essay collection *Tell Me What You Want, What You Really, Really Want* (Stenberg Press/Piet Zwart Institute, 2010) and his writing has appeared in different journals, anthologies and monographs. He plays bass and sings in La Stampa (Staatsakt/Berlin).

What, How & for Whom/WHW

What, How & for Whom/WHW is a curatorial collective formed in 1999 and based in Zagreb, Croatia. Its members are Ivet Ćurlin, Ana Dević, Nataša Ilić and Sabina Sabolović, and designer and publicist Dejan Kršić. WHW organizes a range of production, exhibition and publishing projects and directs Gallery Nova in Zagreb. What, how and for whom, the three basic questions of every economic organisation, concern the planning, concept and realisation of exhibitions as well as the production and distribution of artworks and the artist's position in the labour market. These questions formed the title of WHW's first project dedicated to the 152nd anniversary of the Communist Manifesto, in 2000 in Zagreb, and became the motto of WHW's work and the title of the collective. WHW curated the 11th Istanbul Biennial titled *What Keeps Mankind Alive?* (2009).

Editors' Acknowledgments

We would like to thank all the contributing writers: Julie Ault, Maibritt Borgen, Céline Condorelli, Anthony Davies, Ekaterina Degot, Stephan Dillemuth, Barnaby Drabble, Jonas Ekeberg, Linus Elmes, Charles Esche, Juan A Gaitán, Johan Frederik Hartle, Jakob Jakobsen, Abdellah Karroum, Livia Pancu, David Riff, Jan Verwoert, What, How & for Whom/WHW and the series editor David Blamey for his trust and support.

We would also like to thank BAC – Baltic Art Center, Pauline van Mourik Broekman, Nathan Budzinski, Daniela Castro, Emma Chubb, Eileen Daly, Ann Demeester, Kim Einarsson, Jacob Fabricius, Funen Art Academy, Rebecca Gordon Nesbitt, Kit Hammonds, Eva Rem Hansen, Dóra Hegyi, Niels Henriksen, Hordaland Art Centre-staff, Toril Johannessen, Kaffemisjonen; Bergen, Hassan Khan, Hyunjin Kim, Jang Un Kim, Valentinas Klimašauskas, Krzysztof Kościuczuk, Maria Lind, Bjørn-Henrik Lybeck, Sarat Maharaj, Glenn Jensen Mangerøy, Hallvard Moe, Ingrid Birce Müftüoğlu, Nina Möntmann, Gerrie van Noord, Office for Contemporary Art Norway, Nana Oforiatta-Ayim, Kasper Ostrup, Jet Pascua, David Michael Perez, Raw Material Company, Lisa Rosendahl, Vilde Salhus Røed, Katharina Schlieben, Florian Schneider, S!gnal, Kristina Hagström Ståhl, Jelena Vesić, Mick Wilson, Magdalena Ziółkowska and Didem Özbek for their support and valuable discussions in the process.

A special thanks goes to Arne Skaug Olsen for being instrumental in the initial stages of this anthology project and for supporting it throughout.

Authors' Acknowledgements

Juie Ault's text is an amalgamation of 'Historical Inquiry as Subject and Object', published in *Índex Magazine*, no. 0, autumn 2010, Museu d'Art Contemporani de Barcelona (MACBA), and extracts from *Remembering and Forgetting in the Archive: Instituting 'Group Material'* (1979–96), Doctoral Studies and Research in Fine and Performing Arts Malmö, no. 8, Malmö Lund University, Sweden, 2011.

Anthony Davies, Stephan Dillemuth and Jakob Jakobsen would like to thank Pauline van Mourik Broekman for editorial support.

Linus Elmes wishes to thank Kristina Hagström Ståhl for translation from Swedish to English.

Abdellah Karroum wishes to thank Emma Chubb for translation from French to English. The text *My History of the History of L'appartement 22* is an edited version of the opening keynote lecture for the conference 'Etat des Lieux'/'Condition Report', held in Dakar on 18-20 January 2012 organised by Raw Material Company, and is also a text-in-progress for the book currently under development for the tenth anniversary of L'appartement 22.

Series Editor
David Blamey

Editors
Stine Hebert
Anne Szefer Karlsen

Editors' assistants
Bjørn-Henrik Lybeck
Eva Rem Hansen

Proofing
Gerrie van Noord
Eileen Daly

Design
Jonathan Hares

Design Layout
Joseph Pochodzaj

Font
Stephan Müller
Unica Neue Regular & Light

Cover Paper
Neenah Lahnstein
Neobond 200gsm

Publisher
Open Editions / Hordaland Art Centre

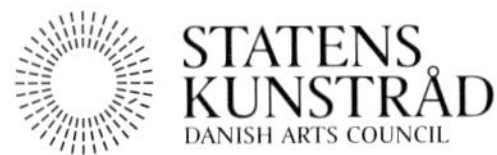

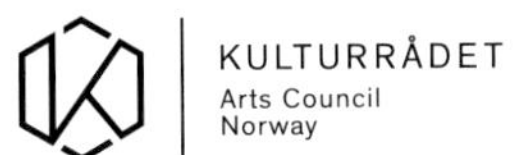

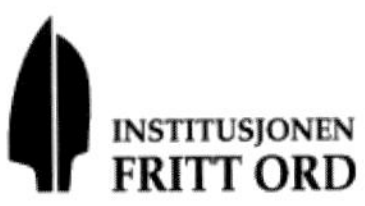

E-orders:
Open Editions
orders@openeditions.com
+44 (0)20 7830 9779

UK Distributor
Art Data
orders@artdata.co.uk
+44 (0)20 8747 1061

European Distributor
Motto
www.mottodistribution.com
+49 (0)30 7544 2119

North American Distributor
DAP (Distributed Art Publishers)
www.artbook.com

Norwegian Distributor
Hordaland Art Centre
ISBN: 978-82-998283-3-8
www.kunstsenter.no

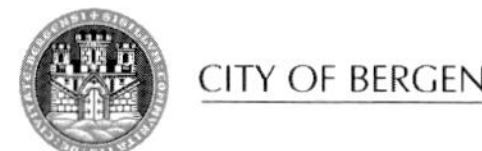

HORDALAND **ART CENTRE**

Occasional Table is an imprint for critical writing on a wide range of themes in contemporary art and culture. Published by Open Editions, new titles will be produced occasionally. This series also includes *Curating and the Educational Turn,* and *Curating Subjects*, both published in collaboration with de Appel Arts Centre in Amsterdam.